TEACHER EVALUATION

Improvement, Accountability,
and Effective Learning

TEACHER EVALUATION

Improvement, Accountability, and Effective Learning

Milbrey Wallin McLaughlin
R. Scott Pfeifer

TEACHERS
COLLEGE
PRESS

Teachers College, Columbia University
New York and London

Published by Teachers College Press, 1234 Amsterdam Avenue,
New York, NY 10027

Library of Congress Cataloging-in-Publication Data

McLaughlin, Milbrey Wallin.
    Teacher evaluation : improvement, accountability, and effective
    learning / Milbrey Wallin McLaughlin, R. Scott Pfeifer.
        p.   cm.
    Bibliography: p. 157
    Includes index.
    ISBN 0-8077-2891-8   ISBN 0-8077-2890-X (pbk.)
    1. Teachers—United States—Rating of.   I. Pfeifer, R. Scott.
II. Title.
LB2838.M385 1988
371.1'44—dc19   87-26101
                                                CIP

Manufactured in the United States of America
93 92 91 90 89 88   1 2 3 4 5 6

Contents

Acknowledgments

A study such as this one is not possible without the interest, cooperation, candor, and support of those individuals who are part of the inquiry. We are indebted to the many administrators and teachers in Santa Clara, Mountain View-Los Altos, Moraga, and Charlotte for their open and insightful responses to our questions about teacher evaluation in their districts—how their programs came to be, their strong and weak points, their accomplishments and shortcomings. The commitment of these individuals to teacher evaluation and to learning from experience is extraordinary.

We also have benefitted from the good sense, wisdom, and critical insight of our Stanford colleagues, Edwin Bridges, Robert Calfee, Larry Cuban, and David Tyack. Each of these professors has strong and active involvement in education policy and practice, and each provided essential reference and review throughout. Nina Bascia, a Stanford School of Education student in Administration and Policy Analysis, provided invaluable research and editorial assistance during the process of revision.

While this project would not have been possible without the support and participation of all these helpful people, they are, of course, in no way responsible for its shortcomings.

The National Institute of Education supported this project through Stanford's Institute for Research on Educational Finance and Governance.

CHAPTER 1

The Teacher Evaluation Problem

Most school districts and state legislatures have wrestled with teacher evaluation. Evaluation of teachers' performance sits at the heart of general concerns about the quality of teachers, the instruction available to youngsters, and educators' accountability for the outcomes of schooling. Teacher evaluation also is central to popular proposals for reform. Initiatives such as merit pay, career ladders, or mentor teacher programs all assume a meaningful, valid system for assessing the performance of teachers.

Legislators, citizens, and local school trustees pushing for more and better teacher evaluation believe it has a major role to play in promoting accountability and in improving the quality of instruction. Teacher evaluation, policymakers and planners expect, can rid the system of "bad apples" by identifying incompetent teachers. And it can contribute to quality education by furnishing feedback on more and less effective classroom practices. Teacher evaluation, in short, is pursued as a potent strategy for enhancing both quality and control of American public education.

THE CYNICISM OF EDUCATORS

Teachers generally share neither this enthusiasm nor these expectations. In state after state, teachers' organization leaders have been vocal opponents of evaluation-based reforms. At the local level, collective bargaining agreements are forged to protect against district teacher evaluation schemes. Most teachers doubt that teacher evaluation can serve either accountability objectives or improvement goals.

Claims for teacher evaluation as an aid to improvement fall on cynical ears. Teacher evaluation, teachers remind policymakers, has no tradition as a strategy to foster improvement. Instead, inspection and control have characterized teacher evaluation activities since colonial times (Peterson, 1982). And at least since the turn of the century, teachers have protested that such appraisals undermine their professional status and misrepresent the teaching task. In 1916, for example, Sara H. Fahey, President of the National Education Association's (NEA) Department of Classroom Teachers, launched a forceful attack on the so-called "efficiency system" as a pernicious and wrong-headed effort to standardize the relationship between individual teachers and students (Peterson, 1982:38). More recent assessments sound the same theme: "Negative perceptions about evaluations and programs have often developed because of poor communications and a feeling that some programs are designed to penalize rather than reward teachers" (Southern Regional Education Board, 1986:2). In a similar vein, a spokesman for the Association for Supervision and Curriculum Development remarked that ". . . preoccupation with trying to build a [teacher evaluation] system that will enable a school to separate the 'good' teachers from the 'bad' and then provide such good 'hard' data that a challenged dismissal case will be successful, has done as much as anything to break down the effectiveness of teacher evaluation" (McGreal, 1983:3).

So while claims for evaluation as an aid to improvement largely go unbelieved, teachers criticize accountability-based plans as misconceived. Teachers argue that the prevailing checklist approach to evaluation, especially those grounded in the process-product model of instruction, is an inappropriate tool for assessing the quality of classroom practices and thus teachers' accountability. Teachers point to a number of fundamental concerns:

- Learner outcomes are cumulative; it is difficult to isolate the effect of any one teacher on a student's performance.
- Teacher behaviors and activities interact with numerous factors to shape student performance. Student socioeconomic status, school climate, pupil abilities, previous instructional treatment, family life and home conditions are but a few of the many factors that influence a student's performance. "Teacher effectiveness," however defined, is highly contextual and conditional.
- Teachers vary enormously in the practices that work for them and the problems they confront in their particular classrooms (Amor et al., 1977; Good, 1983, for example). Good, a long-time student of teacher effectiveness, points out that "One myth that has been discredited by classroom observation is that schooling is a constant experience with

teachers behaving in similar ways and pursuing similar goals with a common curriculum" (1983:418). No single instructional program works for all teachers or for all students; effectiveness depends on the classroom context. Thus there can be "no single, simple method of evaluating teacher effectiveness because there is no single concept of what the teacher should be undertaking in the classroom" (Travers, 1981:22). Most accountability-oriented evaluation systems, in other words, are not "accounting" for the right things and so are bound to be less effective than planners hoped in bringing meaningful control or oversight to the schools.

These substantive disagreements with the form and process of most teacher evaluation strategies underlie teachers' protests that teacher evaluation trivializes the teaching task and erodes the professionalism sought by educators. The rule-based checklists used in most school districts derive their authority from *bureaucratic* forms of control, not professional authority. Teacher evaluation, thus, is perceived to be at odds with goals central to the teaching profession—increased professional stature and increased autonomy for classroom teachers. The former, teachers argue, is their due; the latter, greater responsibility and flexibility in classroom-level decision-making, is essential to improved classroom practice. Enhanced educational quality, teachers assert, requires less administrative control, not more.

Many building-level administrators join teachers in giving low marks to the overall utility of most teacher evaluation schemes. In most school districts teacher evaluation is an irritating administrative burden that accomplishes little and, administrators fear, that risks poisoning otherwise productive working relationships with school staff.

Teacher evaluation proposals thus generate a fundamental dilemma. Proponents, the public and their elected representatives, make legitimate demands for a social report and high-quality public schools. Teacher evaluation is seen as central to these goals. Conversely, educators, especially teachers, resist this rush to more and stronger teacher evaluation. Educators' opposition is rooted in the generally desultory state of present teacher evaluation practices and the view that little in terms of meaningful accountability or improvement can result. Instead, opponents assert, teacher evaluation could actually work against these objectives by decreasing professional autonomy, flexibility, and responsibility.

Both sides thus talk past each other, and the goals of one kind of reform appear to collide with the goals of the other. Policymakers' push for quality and accountability confronts practitioners' push for increased professional autonomy. Demands for greater control by those who support and oversee public education clash with demands for greater responsibility and authority by those who provide public education.

THE NEED FOR ORGANIZATIONAL CHANGE

This book takes up the tension inherent in these two perspectives on teacher evaluation and control. Can accountability coexist with improvement and professional autonomy? Can a single teacher evaluation system meet either end? One central assumption guided the research and analysis presented here: teachers' opinions about evaluation determine its outcome. The effectiveness of any teacher evaluation system—its ability to promote genuine accountability, its ability to contribute valid, reliable information to teachers' improvement—depends finally on the responses of those being evaluated, the teachers. Teachers defensive about the purposes or process of evaluation not surprisingly respond with "show-and-tell" classroom performance rather than with candid discussion of their objectives, strengths and weaknesses, and unrehearsed examples of their classroom activities. Teachers cautious about intent and validity of an evaluation scheme close the classroom door to shield themselves from assessment and view. Teachers fearful of evaluation hide their errors and then hide the fact that they are hiding errors.

This view shifts the focus from technical problems to organizational issues as the primary obstacle to initiating and carrying out meaningful teacher evaluation. In particular, teacher evaluation efforts fail to get off the ground in the first instance because of the absence of trust—trust that the process will be fair, trust that the process will be worthwhile, and trust that the outcome will be of value. These enabling attitudes exist in few schools and districts. Instead, trust between teachers and administrators typically is low; hostility and defensiveness is the norm; communication among actors in the school system characteristically is closed, particularly around issues of evaluation (for example, Herndon, 1985; Lawton et al., 1984). Vertical channels of communication among levels within the district are obstructed by this defensive posture and so often are ignored or heard only selectively (Glidewell and McLean, 1983). Horizontal communication among teachers and administrators is sporadic since both are isolated in their classrooms and schools (see Lortie, 1969).

The consequences of these attitudes and behaviors for teacher evaluation are distancing teachers from the sources of information that could promote learning and examination and unwillingness on the part of all actors to take evaluation seriously. In most districts evaluation is perceived as a no-win activity for all involved, and so becomes just another annoying burden.

Moving from defensiveness to trust, from a self-sealing system to an open system of communication, from norms of hiding mistakes to norms of inquiry and risk-taking, from viewing evaluation as a pro forma necessity to seeing evaluation as a central feature of a school system's organization, poses an *organizational change* problem of the highest order. For most school districts, effecting the organizational conditions necessary for successful introduction and conduct of a strong teacher evaluation system—creating a climate for evaluation—requires change in deeply held values and fundamental modification in the behavioral strategies that characterize institutional activity.

These requirements for change extend far beyond the marginal adjustments sufficient for many change efforts (Berman and McLaughlin, 1978; Sabatier and Mazmanian, 1980). They involve what organizational theorists call the "unfreezing" of an institution's core values, norms, and expectations (Lewin, 1938). The most difficult problem of teacher evaluation, then, is not only to develop a better instrument. It involves organizational questions of getting started—how to overcome the resistance and negative attitudes that exist about teacher evaluation.

This book explores this process of change and the evaluation efforts associated with it. We draw on the experience of four districts to examine the questions of starting and sustaining consequential teacher evaluation practices. Although each district is at a different stage of the process and experiences somewhat different benefits and problems, each also has successfully overcome these initial obstacles to initiate a meaningful teacher evaluation effort.

Teachers' comments about teacher evaluation in the four districts we studied contrast with the sharp, negative responses heard elsewhere.

[Evaluation] is motivating. It keeps me on my toes. You aren't allowed to get sloppy. . . . [Without it] I think I would get in a rut. I'd probably get bored. Evaluation is an incentive that pushes you to improve.

What evaluation [in our district] does is keep you from taking the easy way out and sloughing off on your job. I really think that evaluation is good for education as a whole. To be honest, without evaluation I think my job would be easier. I would not put in as much work as I do now.

Evaluation has an important purpose for everyone. . . . [Without it] I think I might just sit back on my laurels . . . after all I have been teaching for 32 years. At this stage, it would be easy for me to relax. Just like the kids when pressure is taken off, adults can tend to coast, too . . . I think the pressures of evaluation and the expectations it places on you are good.

Even strong teachers need to be challenged every now and then . . . the evaluation process provides a way of looking at teaching in new ways.

Evaluation really has made me much more conscious about how I do things in my classroom. Because of our district's evaluation, I am much more conscious overall about my practice and I think about my lessons more systematically.

I've never had an evaluation this thorough before—it made me feel a bit more worthwhile . . . it really gave me a boost.

I have just finished a year of [evaluation program prescribed] remediation. I am really excited about getting a fresh start next year. I really believe I have to make changes in my teaching behavior, if only for my own happiness.

What kinds of districts and evaluation activities produce these positive reviews of teacher evaluation?

THE DISTRICTS IN BRIEF

The four districts we visited differ in size, resources, management traditions, institutional context for change, and present and past teacher evaluation efforts. They also differ in the stages of development of their teacher evaluation system. However, all four districts have, with varying degrees of success, managed to overcome the negative attitudes associated with teacher evaluation and have made progress in installing teacher evaluation practices that promote both accountability and improvement. The details of each district's experiences with teacher evaluation provide the data for the analysis and argument presented in the chapters that follow. Following is a brief sketch of each district and its teacher evaluation effort.

Santa Clara Unified School District

Approximately 13,000 students in fourteen schools are served by the Santa Clara Unified School District (SCUSD), which lies in the heart of the Silicon Valley south of San Francisco. District enrollment has steadily declined over the past decade, necessitating fifteen school closures and two major district reorganizations. Teachers and community members attribute SCUSD's present fiscal health to the excellent management skills of the superintendent, Rudi Gatti, and the climate of "shared governance" he fosters within the district.

The Santa Clara Unified School District has modeled its teacher evaluation system after that developed in the Salt Lake City Public Schools by former superintendent Donald Thomas (see Wise, Darling-Hammond, McLaughlin, and Bernstein, 1984, for a description of the Salt Lake City strategy). The backbone of the evaluation system is the remediation process to which principals may assign teachers they judge to be performing inadequately. To be referred for formal remediation, teachers must receive a less-than-satisfactory rating for one year, and their principals must demonstrate that they have provided appropriate assistance at the school site.

If referred for formal remediation, the teacher and the assistant superintendent for personnel mutually select two or three teachers to form a remediation team. These individuals have access to any district resources they deem necessary to assist them in supervising the teacher and supporting his or her improvement, including workshops, training materials, and substitute days for observation and conferences. Strict confidentiality is maintained. At the end of the sixty-day remediation period, the team recommends the teacher's continued employment or dismissal. Over the past decade, approximately twenty-six individuals have undergone formal remediation. At the end of the process, one-half of them elected to resign; one-half continued successfully in the classroom.

For the majority of teachers in SCUSD, evaluation is similar to that found in most California school districts. It occurs on a two-year cycle and involves a goal-setting process, a minimum of two classroom observations, and post-conferences. Teachers receive a rating of "effective" or "needs improvement" in each of seven categories of professional competence based on data collected by the principal. In the event of deficiency, the principal constructs an informal remediation program to assist the teachers. Continued deficiency results in a referral for formal remediation.

Attention to teacher evaluation by building administrators has waned recently; for example, only one teacher has been referred for formal remediation over the past two years. The amount of time devoted to evaluation activity varies widely from school to school. Superintendent Gatti attributes this lack of attention to his own failure to make teacher evaluation a priority in the district in recent years. Declining enrollments, fiscal retrenchment, district reorganizations, and curricular reform over the past several years have diverted his attention from teacher evaluation, which he considers nonetheless to be the bedrock of his shared governance approach to district management.

The average age of teachers in SCUSD is fifty-three. Recently, in an effort to address the developmental needs of this veteran workforce and improve the instructional leadership skills of building administrators, the district initiated a comprehensive program of staff development based on Madeline Hunter's instructional theory-into-practice approach. Titled "Effective Instruction and Support" (EIS), the program introduces participants to the theory of lesson design and requires them to put it into practice under the tutelage of a trained coach. Presently, all administrators, including central-office staff, have participated, along with 20% of the district's teachers. Eventually, all teachers will complete the EIS program, which superintendent Gatti hopes can serve as the focus of the district's teacher evaluation program.

Santa Clara Unified School District provides a good example of a particular, well-developed approach to evaluation: peer-based remediation. In addition, the experience of this district permits us to examine the systematic effects of uneven administrative attention to an established teacher evaluation strategy.

Mountain View–Los Altos
Union High School District

The Mountain View-Los Altos Union High School District enrolls approximately 3,000 students in two high schools located in an affluent community, which straddles the Silicon Valley area in the San Francisco bay area. Approximately 75% of these students attend college upon graduation, and their achievement test scores are well above California averages.

Ever since the passage more than a decade ago of the state's Stull Act, a bill requiring local school districts to evaluate teachers, Mountain View-Los Altos has approached the topic of teacher evaluation in both a serious and experimental manner. In the 1970s, teachers engaged in collegial evaluation. They also developed a survey form by which students could evaluate their teachers. The initiation of collective bargaining within the district brought an end to collegial evaluation, but the student survey, many times revised, still serves as one of several sources of data administrators use in evaluating teacher performance.

Multiple sources of information about teachers' performance, coupled with a tight linkage to district staff development efforts, define Mountain View-Los Altos's teacher evaluation system. Teachers begin the biannual evaluation cycle by setting instructional goals consistent with district standards and the content of recent district-wide staff-development programs. Three classroom observations coupled with post-conferences provide partial documentation of the teacher's success or failure to attain stated goals. Other sources of data include:

- student survey results from two of the teacher's classes
- grading distributions, which are compared across grade level and departments
- student work samples submitted by the teacher
- teacher-made products such as worksheets and tests
- additional material jointly agreed to by teacher and their prime evaluator.

Evaluators employ their own judgment in weighting this data; no standard formula is used. Administrators assemble the available data at year's end and construct lengthy, narrative, final reports which assess the teacher's strengths and weaknesses on the chosen objectives. Conclusions and recommendations must be rigorously documented.

The district has supported administrators in developing their evaluative skill by devoting a substantial portion of each year's week-long administrative workshop over the past nine years to evaluation topics. Recently, the district secured a grant from a local foundation to design and implement a series of staff-development workshops keyed to the evaluation system. Based on an analysis of recent teacher evaluation reports, the district offered six different workshops, taught by Mountain View-Los Altos teachers, on topics ranging from classroom management to the development of higher-order thinking skills. Staff development and teacher evaluation remain tightly coordinated within the district.

The superintendent, Paul Sakamoto, considers evaluation the

number one administrative priority in the district and backs up this belief by personally observing over 90% of Mountain View's teachers each year, as well as reading and commenting on every teacher evaluation report produced by administrators.

Over the past eight years, twenty-nine unsatisfactory evaluations have been given to eighteen teachers within the district, which represents approximately 7% of the teaching workforce. Ten of these individuals were induced to resign voluntarily, with the remainder following remediation plans coupled with local staff-development efforts that enabled them to earn a satisfactory rating on a subsequent evaluation. Recently, however, relations between administrators and teachers have become strained, in part because of increased district-level emphasis on due process and the legal aspects of teacher evaluation. The Mountain View experience thus provides an important example of an evaluation strategy built on multiple sources of information, including student reports, and also furnishes insight about the effects of an apparent shift in district-level focus from improvement to accountability.

Moraga School District

The Moraga School District is a small, elementary-school district composed of two elementary schools and one intermediate school which together serve 1,400 students. Parents in this bedroom community outside of Oakland, California, play an active role in their children's education. The local education foundation annually raises over $70,000 in private funds to support Moraga's schools, and over 200 parents serve as volunteers during the school day to support instructional efforts.

Prior to the arrival of the current superintendent, Judith Glickman, teachers and building administrators within the district viewed teacher evaluation as a punitive, biased tool used selectively to deny teachers merit salary increments in their eighteenth and twenty-third years of service. Evaluation was a source of dissatisfaction for all and contributed to an overall climate of distrust and poor communication between teachers, the school board, and district administrators.

Glickman set out to construct a positive, instructional climate within the district by conducting personal interviews with every teacher in the district on a yearly basis. She involved building administrators as part of her management team and solicited participation in district decision-making. Most importantly, she tackled the problem of declining teaching effectiveness not through the district's merit-pay provision but through a district-wide staff development initiative that she coupled with a revised teacher evaluation system.

Moraga teachers and administrators taught their peers the lesson design theories of Madeline Hunter in a week-long workshop held for two consecutive summers. Concurrently, administrators received clinical supervision training. Combining both programs enabled administrators and teachers to discuss the elements of instructional effectiveness in concrete terms and to engage in a process of evaluation that focused on improvement. In contrast to past informal evaluation practices, the current system is more formalized, and administrators are held strictly accountable for evaluation results. Preobservation conferences are now standard, written script-tapes accompany each observation, and principals carefully plan post-conferences, which set expectations for future performance.

Declining enrollments have forced many teacher layoffs in recent years in Moraga, but the number of involuntary layoffs has been reduced due to Glickman's efforts to make teacher evaluation and accountability an improvement tool as well. Over the past four years, 10% of the district's teachers have been induced to resign as a direct result of evaluative feedback coupled with district-wide staff-development efforts. And rather than produce dissatisfaction in the remaining teachers, the last four years have brought about a marked increase in teachers' perceptions of the fairness of evaluation. Relations between teachers and administrators in the district are at an all time high.

Moraga contributes important perspective on the problems of initiating a teacher evaluation program, especially in the context of unfavorable organizational conditions and the attendant problems of changing fundamental attitudes and beliefs about the role of evaluation and the priorities of administrators. In many ways, Moraga represents the most "typical" case of teacher evaluation reform examined in this book.

Charlotte–Mecklenburg Schools

The Charlotte-Mecklenburg Schools (CMS), a large, urban public system, serves approximately 72,000 students who live in the city of Charlotte, North Carolina, and surrounding Mecklenburg County. The district may be best known for its model approach to desegregation more than a decade ago, and this spirit of pride and progressivism still pervades the system. More recently, Charlotte achieved notoriety for its commitment to staff-development training (see Schlechty and Crowell, 1982), and these efforts culminated in the design and implementation of a model career-ladder program for teachers entitled "The Career Development Program." The program incorporates staff development, teacher evaluation, and curriculum development in a comprehensive program of professional growth, career advancement, and incentive pay designed to both attract and retain effective teachers.

Impending action by the North Carolina legislature on a statewide merit-pay plan for teachers prompted Charlotte superintendent Jay Robinson to charge a committee of local teachers, administrators, parents, and business leaders to investigate the concept and its implications at the local level. Convinced that merit pay, as currently conceived, would be detrimental to Charlotte teachers and students, the committee, under the leadership of Phillip Schlechty, Professor of Education at the University of North Carolina, Chapel Hill, recommended the development of a comprehensive plan for professional growth which incorporated career stages of increasing responsibility, rigorous performance evaluation, and incentive pay, and which would draw upon the district's demonstrated commitment to staff development. The major innovation in the proposed Career Development Program involved a unique approach to evaluation, and a steering committee composed of teachers, administrators, and union officials began a year-long process of soliciting teacher and community input and support for a radical redesign of professional responsibility within the district.

Participation in the Career Development Program is voluntary for experienced teachers, but all new recruits must join. New teachers are referred to as "provisional teachers," and those experienced volunteers chosen to participate in the first year are known as "career candidates." Evaluating the teacher's performance is the primary responsibility of a school-based committee called an advisory/assistance team, composed of the principal, the assistant principal for instruction (API), and a fellow teacher. For provisional teachers, the fellow teacher is assigned, acting as a mentor. These individuals meet periodically with the teachers, helping them to construct a program of professional improvement, called an "Action Growth Plan," and brokering available staff-development resources to support them in achieving this plan. The advisory/assessment team also conducts periodic formal and informal observations of the teachers' classroom performance, using the Carolina Teaching Performance Assessment Scale (CTPAS) as the basic evaluation tool. At the end of each semester, the advisory/assistance team reviews data collected to document the teachers' performance and arrives at a summative rating.

This is only a partial picture, however, because a basic principle undergirding the evaluation system is that reliability only results when multiple evaluations are conducted by numerous individuals employing multiple and explicit criteria over a long period of time. Thus, two additional components of evaluation remain. First, the district employs nine specially trained, system-wide observer/evaluators who conduct both announced and unannounced classroom observations employing the CTPAS. These individuals then pass their data on to the advisory/assistance team, serving as an external "validity and reliability check" of their deliberations.

Finally, the summative judgments of a teacher's competence produced by the advisory/assistance teams are subject to the review and confirmation of both a regional and district-wide committee composed of teachers and administrators before advancement along the career ladder is granted.

Supporting career development is now the focus of district staff-development efforts. Provisional teachers receive training in classroom management skills and the elements of effective lesson design. Career candidates receive training tailored to the content of their action growth plan. Release time is granted to mentors and provisional teachers to enable them to plan and discuss areas of need.

Charlotte's Career Development Program had been operational only for one year at the time we visited. Thus, it is difficult to assess its impact at this time. Standards for advancement, however, appear to be high. Of 150 career candidates nominated by their peers as outstanding teachers, only 137 were advanced to Career Level I status, with the remaining thirteen either choosing to drop out of the program or participate for another year. Even in its early stages, however, Charlotte provides rich data about experience with designing and implementing a district-wide reform, about the operation of multiple evaluation activities, and about the problems associated with developing comprehensive reform, or as Schlechty quips, about "building an airplane while in flight."

SUMMARY

These districts are not "lighthouse" districts with a history of well-supported innovation and development. Nor are they all small, wealthy, or homogeneous—characteristics often asserted as necessary to initiating a consequential teacher evaluation program. Instead, their particular context and characteristics generated a particular approach to evaluation, one that fits the demands, tenor, and style of the setting.

But how did they get started? How did they proceed to their present level of development with teacher evaluation? These four districts began with little more appetite for strong teacher evaluation than exists in most districts across the country. The critical differences, as we will see, lie in *how* these quite diverse districts went about addressing the issue of teacher evaluation.

From our research, then, we will describe a process of individual and organizational change whereby school districts can move from ritualistic pro forma teacher evaluation to meaningful assessment of teachers' performance. Through a single evaluation system, schools are, in fact, building programs able to serve both accountability and improvement goals. The experiences of these districts suggest that the dilemma between policymakers' concerns for accountability and practitioners' concerns for professionalism are not unresolvable.

CHAPTER 2

Enabling Teacher Evaluation

If you want to understand something, try changing it.
—Kurt Lewin

Undertaking significant teacher evaluation means undertaking significant organizational change. And it is change of a particular sort. Meaningful teacher evaluation requires more than simply adding a bit of this and a bit of that to existing practices. It requires changes in the deeply held beliefs and understandings that accompany accounting, monitoring, and judging if teachers are to be sufficiently candid and open and if administrators are to be sufficiently attentive. Teacher evaluation necessarily engages fundamental concerns—the value, quality, and effectiveness of an educator's work. Teacher evaluation also engages core institutional issues such as allocation of human and fiscal resources, role conflicts between administrators as managers and administrators as colleagues, and the generation of information about the performance of the institution. These concerns and issues are not trivial. Indeed, what is more surprising than general absence of consequential teacher evaluation practices around the country is the fact that useful teacher evaluation is happening at all.

The significance of values and expectations to the outcome of a teacher evaluation frames the problem of organizational change. That is, teacher evaluation is difficult to bring about in large part because planners and reformers cannot mandate what matters most. Mandates for strong teacher evaluation, or even the installation of new evaluation practices, do not necessarily have much to do with the norms and understandings that determine how teachers and administrators treat teacher evaluation.

Getting started with teacher evaluation, then, is not a question of making or willing it to happen. At base, it is a question of *enabling* it to happen—of developing the necessary trust, communication, openness, and commitment to strong evaluation. These are the enabling conditions that establish the local *evaluation culture*. For example, Charlotte's Phillip Schlechty used similar terms when he described his district's efforts to

15

move from ritualistic to substantive teacher evaluation as a culture-building exercise:

> Developing an evaluative culture around which everything else will hang is really difficult, but that must be our focus. The problems [associated with implementation] will disappear and not be problems anymore if we just stick to this culture-building exercise.

To varying degrees, each of the institutions we observed moved from organizational conditions unfriendly to evaluation to an institutional climate that supports strong teacher evaluation. The specific change problem confronting each district reflected its particular context, characteristics, and traditions. Thus the processes and activities associated with change in each district varied. However, common elements characterized each district's efforts to develop a culture or enabling conditions for teacher evaluation and to inform the general problem of getting started.

TRIGGERING EVENT

Some kind of event jolted actors and policy in each district and began the organizational process of "unfreezing" the environment in preparation for serious consideration of teacher evaluation. Willingness to consider basic change stands in contrast to the dynamic conservativism that characterizes most school districts and other organizational settings (Schon, 1971). Change, when it occurs, typically is incremental only and is directed at maintaining organizational status quo through marginal adjustments to existing practice. Organizational change of this sort constitutes little more than running to stay in place; it does not engage the organization's fundamental norms, values, or technologies (Meyer and Rowan, 1977). Incremental change is insufficient to promoting the enabling conditions of trust and open communication necessary for effective teacher evaluation.

But more than incremental change is hard to bring about unless there is a "triggering event" to shock the system and force individuals to examine processes and issues basic to the institution. A triggering event also supports significant change because it makes it possible for someone within the system to violate existing rules and norms with relative safety (Schon, 1971; Argyris, 1982; Lundberg, 1985). Unless accepted ways of "doing things around here" can be examined and challenged, incremental or marginal change is an expected outcome.

A triggering event—which might take the form of internal managerial crises, new leadership, or externally imposed pressure on the system—can momentarily suspend routines and launch the institutional process of change. But just as data relies on an analyst to provide significance, events such as these rely on individual initiative and vision to function as a strategic trigger for basic change. An event must be seized as an occasion to challenge previously unquestioned values, assumptions, and behaviors (Lundberg, 1985).

The districts we studied show how disparate triggers can begin a process of organizational change. State action prompted rethinking of teacher evaluation strategies in Charlotte and Mountain View-Los Altos. In Charlotte, impending state action regarding merit pay caused the superintendent to form a committee to study the concept. Fear that the state might impose a merit-pay system inconsistent with the district's management philosophy spurred efforts to design a career development program. Central-office administrators saw the new state policy as a significant threat to local autonomy and control: "If we couldn't come up with some kind of solution to the teacher quality problem, then the state was going to impose something on us."

New state-level policy of a different sort pushed Mountain View-Los Altos into action. This district had been experimenting for several years with various models for evaluating teachers, some of which involved peer review. Passage of a state collective bargaining law presented a dilemma—neither the union nor the district administration felt that existing teacher evaluation practices were consistent with a collective bargaining framework. According to a union official,

> When it became clear that evaluation would have some meaningful consequences attached to it, such as dismissal, well, that's when [the district] decided it wasn't our proper role to be involved, and we agreed.

Current evaluation practices in Mountain View-Los Altos thus trace their origins to the beginning of formal collective bargaining within the district and the fundamental rethinking this state-level initiative occasioned.

In Moraga and Santa Clara, change in district leadership coupled with external pressures provoked fundamental changes in district routines. Declining enrollments, the necessity to lay off teachers in the district, and the arrival of Judith Glickman as Moraga's superintendent combined to stimulate reform. From the day she arrived, Glickman set about to alter basic district management patterns and expectations. Her management style contrasted sharply with that of the previous superintendent. According to one school board member:

> The former superintendent was an administrator—he was as isolated as a person. He was not open or outward or able to take resistance. It was just his personality . . . Judy—she is totally different. Now, the walls are really breaking down. . . . Now, the word is that everybody can be a better teacher.

A new superintendent coupled with the imperative to deal with sharp enrollment declines and an impending school closure made change inevitable in Moraga. Glickman exploited the break in organizational routines presented by the change of leadership to challenge traditional operations. And teacher evaluation lay at the heart of the new superintendent's strategy for quality improvement in Moraga.

Similarly, in Santa Clara, change in leadership provided the occasion for fundamental shift in organizational routines. A new superintendent, combined with a breakdown in communication at all levels of the school system, led to the initiation of fundamental teacher evaluation reform. In 1974, the new superintendent, Rudi Gatti, expressed a strong commitment to building consensus among district constituencies and promoting open communication. This management stance departed radically from the closed-door management techniques that fueled past union-management problems. As Gatti put it:

> In the early '70s, the teachers' association and the board had a terrible relationship, and they were playing hardball with one another. All they were doing was finding fault with each other . . . and this resulted in a backlash where people tried to find fault with the teaching staff. . . . When I came to the district, I said to the Board, "We need to bridge the gap between us and open up communications."

Gatti seized the catalytic potential in a leadership shift and, as a former director of personnel, chose teacher evaluation as the focal point for his plan.

In each site, then, some event functioned as a trigger to disrupt traditional attitudes and behaviors and to force consideration of fundamental change in organizational practices. Respondents in each district underscore the event's strategic value and agree that little change in evaluation practices could have occurred without it. Other experiences underscore the importance of this component. For example, the organizational change processes described in the Rand Corporation's examination of teacher evaluation (Wise et al., 1984) also were set in motion by an event that jarred the system—in Toledo, Ohio, impending bankruptcy compelled teachers to propose a new, strong system of performance assessment; in Salt Lake City, Utah, sharp enrollment declines threatened teachers' jobs and prompted agreement about a strategy for professional accountability; in Lake Washington, Washington State, dismissal of a superintendent and community censure of the school board paved the way fo a new superintendent's proposals for substantively new policies, with teacher evaluation at the core.

Yet, a triggering event is far from a sufficient condition for initiating evaluation reform or any kind of fundamental change. For example, to our knowledge, Charlotte-Mecklenburg is the only district in North Carolina that embarked on a reform program with teacher evaluation at its center in response to the state-level merit-pay proposals. And superintendents come and go in California as they do in districts across the country. The events we described served as triggers for change because district leaders transformed them into a mandate for change.

Events such as those that precipitated action in the sites we examined served as catalysts for change only because leadership chose to use them that way. Thus the event provided a necessary occasion to infringe established norms and practices and to mobilize interest in change. But the experiences of the districts we visited also suggests that a triggering event must be accompanied by some kind of district-level activity that legitimizes attention to teacher evaluation and sets the stage for teachers' reconsideration of the worth of a consequential evaluation.

LEGITIMIZING ACTIVITIES

Most educators and district officials have been allergic to traditional forms of teacher evaluation. They have argued, with basis in fact, that teacher evaluation is inappropriate, insensitive, and a waste of time. Thus claims about the value of teacher evaluation as a tool for either professional accountability or improvement often are heard with little more credibility than are claims that "the check is in the mail." It is one thing, then, to open the institution to reexamination of basic assumptions and routines. It is quite another thing to mobilize support for teacher evaluation. Teachers (and administrators) require more than a shock to the system to lend their support to substantive teacher evaluation.

And, in fact, we saw that the triggering event in each district was accompanied by activities that legitimized attention to evaluation and engendered teachers' support for developing meaningful teacher evaluation. Although specific legitimizing activities varied by district, they shared a common feature—a highly visible, comprehensive, and district-wide focus on improvement.

Moraga's superintendent invested heavily in staff-development programs and clinical training, establishing clear district priority for improvement. Teacher evaluation was addressed only after these staff-development activities had been underway for two years; evaluation became the logical next step in the district's overall plan. Charlotte's innovative Career Development Program, adopted with the strong support of teachers, is built upon a comprehensive evaluation plan. Charlotte teachers were pushed to accept this strong teacher evaluation role by the perception that the school board was concerned about the apparent shortage of qualified teachers and that no more across-the-board pay raises would be voted until teacher evaluation was tackled in a fundamental way. In Santa Clara, teacher evaluation was a central part of the "shared governance" model adopted to improve the quality of education in the district. Similarly, in Mountain View-Los Altos, evaluation was framed in the context of the superintendent's express commitment to training and staff development.

In each of these districts, then, teacher evaluation was a component of a broader effort to improve district practices and derived legitimacy from this association. Neither accountability nor improvement functioned as stand-alone concepts; they were embedded in district-wide activities for which evaluation had a clear, positive, and central purpose.

LEADERSHIP

Making all this happen—transforming events into triggers for organizational change and giving teacher evaluation legitimacy—depends critically and absolutely on district leadership. Nothing of significance will happen in the area of teacher evaluation unless the superintendent demands it. District superintendents are key actors in teacher evaluation reform for many reasons. They not only marshal resources for teacher evaluation; they also serve an important symbolic function by focusing attention on teacher evaluation, making it a priority and establishing the climate within which it can occur (Bridges, 1986; Wise et al., 1984).

In order for teacher evaluation to become a long-term priority in any district, it must be at the heart of the superintendent's vision for quality improvement. For example, Mountain View-Los Altos's superintendent Sakamoto sees evaluation as a critical lever for student achievement and instructional improvement:

> Evaluation is key to any comprehensive program in a school district . . . as far as I'm concerned, evaluation is the key to what goes on in the district. Prior to our reforms in recent years, evaluation was just a cursory affair. It was just an exercise of turning in forms to the central office. It did nothing to ensure that good instruction was going on in the district. . . . If the key to student achievement is really what goes on in the classroom, then we certainly ought to be focusing our time and attention here. So often teachers feel isolated. They feel nobody cares what goes on in their classroom and they just close the door. Evaluation has opened up the door and has provided a way to get into the classes and allow colleagues to share what is going on.

Glickman, in Moraga, states her philosophy similarly:

> Staff development articulates what is appropriate instruction. . . . Formal evaluation serves to get someone's attention—it raises their level of concern and can be used to prove fairness to other teachers.

In Charlotte, the Career Development Program represented the culmination of an almost decade-long commitment to staff-development training which was crafted out of superintendent Robinson's vision for the district.

But superintendents must successfully articulate their vision for teacher evaluation for it to take root. Their outward and explicit commitment is essential to commanding the attention of principals and other building-level administrators assigned evaluation responsibilities. Teacher evaluation competes with many other demands for building administrators' time; it also poses a fundamental role conflict for principals who fear that evaluation and support for development are incompatible. Teacher evaluation becomes a priority for middle managers only if it is a visible, active priority for the superintendent who effectively communicates this desire through the chain of command. A Charlotte assistant principal puts it this way:

> We put [our] emphasis where our superiors put the emphasis. The principal [in this building] has made [teacher evaluation] a top priority [because] the superintendent [and the area superintendent for this school] says it's a top priority.

Further, the importance of top-level concern is not a one-time or short-term thing. Santa Clara Unified School District illustrates how a lapse in a superintendent's express attention to teacher evaluation can undermine the process—even when it is apparently established. The district's national recognition for successful handling of the problems associated with enrollment decline and fiscal retrenchment has been well deserved, but distraction of the superintendent's attention from teacher evaluation has been one side effect of this crisis. Principals' attention to teacher evaluation is demonstrably uneven throughout the district, and only one teacher has been placed on remediation in the past two years. Gatti explains the apparent erosion in teacher evaluation this way:

> My attention has really been elsewhere in the past several years. . . . The problem is that it's difficult to keep the fire burning for a lot of people. . . . I'm just going to have to get out into the schools and push them into paying more attention to evaluation.

Superintendents signaled their priority for and commitment to teacher evaluation in a number of ways. For example, superintendent Sakamoto and his Director of Curriculum and Instruction, Robert Madgic, read all of the teacher evaluations submitted by district principals; superintendent Sakamoto evaluates his principals on how well they evaluate teachers. Central-office administrators in Mountain View-Los Altos also use mandatory administrator training sessions as a forum for evaluation. Robert Madgic explains:

> We constantly try to focus the administrator's attention of evaluation. We point to the problems of evaluation at principals' meetings. Evaluation is

a topic at every one of these weekly meetings. We have emphasized evaluation for the past eight summers in our administrative workshops in an effort to [build skills] and point out problems with the evaluation process.

Glickman in Moraga adopted an identical strategy to that employed in Mountain View-Los Altos to display her commitment to teacher evaluation, and Santa Clara's Gatti plans to renew his commitment in a similar way. Gatti states:

When something like evaluation stops being the top priority of the person at the top, it starts to fall away. I told my management team this year, however, that teacher evaluation is going to be my number one area of concern next year . . . I'm going to have to get out to all the schools . . . and push them into paying more attention to evaluation. . . . One thing I've already made clear is that all evaluations, both teachers' and administrators', are going to cross my desk next year, and I'm going to initial all of them.

In Charlotte, the multiple district resources Jay Robinson assigned to teacher evaluation provide strong evidence of his commitment to thorough-going, meaningful teacher evaluation. Career development remained the leading agenda item of the district's management committee for over a year. He modified the job description of area program specialists so that they now spend the majority of their time on issues revolving around teacher evaluation. His top-level advisors now meet in a weekly "executive committee" which primarily addresses career development concerns.

Superintendents do more than provide the leadership that establishes teacher evaluation as a priority and focuses administrative attention for it. Even more critically, they create the institutional climate within which teacher evaluation occurs. In order for a district to move from a condition of a low-trust, low-risk-taking organization to one in which teacher evaluation can support meaningful change, channels of communication within the district must be open both vertically and horizontally.

Change in these institutional norms and expectations is not a responsibility to be delegated. Only the superintendent, as the institution's formal leader, can break the cycle of distancing from evaluation and assessment, of disconnectedness from sources of information about performance, and of distrust among organizational roles. Organizational research shows that when an organization's leader is distant and closed, the result is increased bureaucratization and reliance on "rules," so that discontinuities among units and individuals are heightened (Argyris, 1982). Meaningful teacher evaluation is not possible in such a climate.

Unless the organization's leader develops a style of operation that stresses openness and inquiry, little of consequence is likely to happen in the area of teacher evaluation. As our study sites illustrate, when the leader does move from a primarily closed to a more open management style, the organization becomes open to influence and in greater control of its internal activities. And when this happens, opportunities for learning—such as teacher evaluation—become important and possible.

Within each district we examined, open and honest communication and access at all levels of the organization mirrored this management principle. In Charlotte, union leaders praised Superintendent Robinson for his openness and involvement of teachers in district policy formation. Indeed, one attested to the fact that with Robinson as superintendent, collective bargaining was virtually unnecessary. Teachers and administrators in Charlotte also emphasized Robinson's fairness and active style. One administrator commented, "You won't find a more open superintendent than Jay Robinson . . . he is open to a fault. . . . If he has a goal, he says what it is. He hides nothing." Another central office administrator stressed Robinson's activism:

> Jay Robinson . . . is the only manager that comes close in my mind to typifying the principles put forward in *In Search of Excellence*. He has a bias for action. He's a risktaker. He doesn't cover things up but finds answers to problems. He's a gentle man who talks tough and a tough man who talks gently both at the same time. It depends on the situation and what it calls for. His philosophy is to train winners. . . . Failure means you made a bad personnel decision.

Each of the other superintendents in our study demonstrated their commitment to an open management style as well. In Moraga, Glickman takes the time to hold personal conferences with each of the nearly sixty professional staff members in her district each year in an effort to foster communication. Sakamoto in Mountain View-Los Altos makes a point of accessibility and visibility. For example, whenever possible he spends lunchtime at one of the district's schools out in the courtyard talking with teachers and students. Teachers in the district see this style both as unusual and as evidence of a professionally based management style:

. . . there are not many districts where the superintendent comes and sits in the quad at lunchtime and talks to the kids and teachers. We run things on a first-name basis in this district . . . we certainly don't operate on a command model here.

Superintendent Gatti likewise prides himself on the fact that he and his central-office staff rarely close their doors. Open communication lies at the heart of his management strategy. He addresses the staff at each of the district's nineteen schools every year and gathers feedback regarding district programs.

Nothing quite substitutes for personal attention to underscore commitment. Thus, face-to-face contact between central-office administrators and district staff emerged as a critical strategy for promoting open communication. As Charlotte's Phillip Schlechty quipped, "Management by memo really stinks." Face-to-face contact serves several important functions. It is an important "rumor control" strategy, since personal visits by central-office staff is an effective way to uncover misunderstandings and anxieties in the district about teacher evaluation, to respond on the spot, and to collect information about site-level responses to district plans which can sharpen planning or policies.

For example, in Moraga, Glickman's yearly, personal interviews with each teacher in the district helped to avoid misunderstandings regarding the district's new focus on evaluation. In many cases, in fact, she reported that it was in these interviews that she learned of the frustration and unhappiness with teaching many of the district's poorest teachers experienced. This knowledge enabled her to assist these individuals in either improving or changing their careers while still maintaining their self-respect and professional pride. Glickman views her face-to-face contact with teachers as a cornerstone of her evaluation strategy.

Face-to-face contact also provides incontrovertible evidence of central-office priority for evaluation. Respondents in all the districts we studied underscored the importance of personal involvement by the superintendent. This Mountain View-Los Altos teacher's comment is typical:

> The superintendent visits every classroom in the district. It gives a teacher a sense of importance when people feel what they're doing is important enough for him to drop in to see how its going. . . .

The openness we observed between superintendent and teachers—whether in a large or a small school district—was the result of hard work.

Each superintendent cultivated this relationship with both teachers and board members in their districts; they self-consciously sought to break the cycle of distance, disconnectedness, and lack of trust. And in so doing, they displayed leadership of a particular, critical sort necessary for developing strong teacher evaluation.

TEACHER INVOLVEMENT

Evaluation denotes power and control. In most districts, that power is vested totally in the hands of evaluators. Yet our district-based research as well as research in organizations generally demonstrate two important points relevant to teacher evaluation: (1) unilateral power or control is seldom seen as valid by individuals subject to it; (2) those so controlled are unlikely to engage in public testing or experimentation or other possibly threatening activities associated with an effective response to evaluation findings. Involving teachers in the design and implementation of a teacher evaluation system is essential to establishing an "evaluation culture." Indeed, Sakamoto in Mountain View points to teacher involvement as the single most important thing for a district to do as it begins to reform its teacher evaluation system:

> I would involve people from the beginning, and that means teachers. If I was going to start over again, I'd have teachers go and visit sites where evaluation was taking place and talk with teachers there to find out what teachers in that district feel about evaluation. Let's face it. You can't argue with any system that's objective and fair.

Teacher involvement is essential to this perception, and teachers in Charlotte give strong support to this view. They single out teacher involvement as the main reason why "things are so good in Charlotte." A representative from one of Charlotte-Mecklenburg's teachers' associations said, for example,

> . . . the answer [to why new evaluation practices seem to be working Charlotte] is teacher input. We were involved all the way. It is true that mistakes have been made . . . and there is a need to be flexible, but the bottom line is that when teachers are being heard, success is possible.

But the experiences of the districts we examined illustrate that effective teacher involvement is not as straightforward a proposition as it may seem. Forming a committee of teachers and administrators to discuss and recommend changes in existing teacher evaluation policies falls far short of the kind of involvement necessary to secure commitment to the change effort. All teachers in the school district, not just union representatives or volunteers, must be given an opportunity to offer input. To foster commitment, teachers must believe that their involvement will result in substantive change, making the endeavor worth their time.

The districts we visited accomplished the goal of effective teacher involvement with varying degrees of success. Given its size, Charlotte-Mecklenburg faced the most complex task of securing input from over 4,000 professional staff members as they set out to construct the Career Development Program. A central steering committee composed of teachers, union representatives, administrators, and board members directed the planning effort. Each school elected a liaison teacher to serve as a channel for information to and from the steering committee. These individuals came together once a month at district expense to provide input to the actions of the steering committee and take information back to the schools. Seven full-time district-wide liaison teachers canvassed all schools on a regular basis, meeting informally with teachers, explaining the planning process, and soliciting input. Schlechty, the steering committee chair, held public meetings at every school in the district to answer questions and elicit feedback. Anonymous question boxes were placed at each school, and answers to all questions were distributed on a district-wide basis.

Charlotte's strategy for securing participation in the development phase apparently was successful. According to steering committee members, "Everyone who wanted to have input into the planning process had the opportunity." An elementary-school teacher and career candidate corroborated this point: "I watched the planning process closely. I just don't see how the whole developmental process could have had more teacher input." Teacher involvement was particularly meaningful because concrete evidence existed that district officials were listening. For example, specific changes in the selection process for observer/evaluators and first-year career candidates came about as a direct result of teacher suggestions. Throughout the steering committee's deliberations, teachers had the opportunity through their elected liaison to monitor the direction of planning efforts and actually see the Career Development Program take form.

Charlotte's experience also underscores both the importance and the difficulty of sustaining meaningful involvement of teachers through the implementation phase. Despite the generally successful efforts to involve teachers during the planning phase, we encountered numerous examples of misunderstandings about how the teacher evaluation system would operate and how decisions regarding a teacher's status would be made. For some, only seeing is believing. Other teachers and building administrators indicated that teacher input into the implementation process had decreased when compared to the design phase of the previous year. Thus, several individuals, including union representatives, expressed concern for the future. Charlotte's efforts clearly demonstrate the difficulties involved in providing sufficient teacher involvement to secure commitment for the teacher evaluation system by all stakeholders.

In contrast to Charlotte's generally high level of teacher involvement in planning, the level of teacher participation varied considerably in the other three districts. In Mountain View-Los Altos, though teacher involvement in the design of the student survey several years ago was high, many teachers believe that their opportunity for input has been limited in recent years. Teachers unanimously felt the need to reexamine the use of the student survey as part of the formal evaluation process. According to one teacher who has always received satisfactory evaluations:

> . . . the student survey causes such wide-spread discomfort, I wonder if it's worth it. . . . If the student survey is weighted heavily, as a lot of administrators do, how accurate really is it as a measure of a teacher's competence? We're just asking students to do things that they're not qualified to do.

Despite vocal teacher dissatisfaction, district administrators reportedly have been unwilling to reexamine this evaluation strategy.

Both teachers and administrators in the district voiced contradictory opinions regarding the amount of input teachers have had in constructing the current evaluation process. Several teachers and administrators judged the opportunity for input as high. A greater number felt that opportunities for input were sorely lacking. For example, one department head stated:

> Any revision of evaluation should start with the teachers. . . . If instructional improvement is really the objective . . . then you have to ask teachers, "What can we do to set up a system of visitation and observation that would help you the most?" This didn't happen here.

As a counterexample, however, teachers in the district recently developed a set of criteria that would describe excellent teaching in the district. These will be used in conjunction with the evaluation system. In sum, perceptions regarding the level of teacher input into evaluation reform in Mountain View-Los Altos appears to be mixed.

In Moraga, teachers had limited involvement in initial planning stages of a new teacher evaluation system. The district management team alone made many of the decisions regarding the direction teacher evaluation reform would take. One result of the limited involvement of teachers in both Moraga and Mountain View-Los Altos is that teacher acceptance of and commitment to teacher evaluation has come slowly and unevenly. For example, several teachers in both districts felt that evaluation was "something for administrators to do that had little meaning for classroom teachers." These responses suggest that lack of involvement in the planning process limits ownership on the part of teachers.

Our interviews in Santa Clara also illustrate the role teacher involvement plays in securing teacher commitment to the evaluation process. Teacher evaluation holds little salience for many of the teachers and administrators in the district at this time. Notable exceptions, however, are those individuals who had just served on a district-wide committee that revised the year-end evaluation form, along with those actively involved as instructors for the district-wide staff-development program which certified administrators as competent evaluators. Each of these individuals displayed a high level of commitment to teacher evaluation which was not evident in other respondents. Involvement in the planning and implementation process and ownership appear to go hand in hand.

But we saw that teacher involvement in the evaluation has another critical dimension. It is important at the institutional level, as district policy is developed and implemented. But it also is important during the evaluation process itself, at the individual level, as teachers set their goals. In many respects, the negative consequences of lack of involvement at the district level in Moraga and Mountain View-Los Altos are offset by the latitude teachers are given in setting the goals and objectives on which they will be evaluated during the year. According to one Mountain View-Los Altos veteran of nineteen years,

I think the fact that the evaluator and evaluatee had a chance to negotiate and review their goals is an important part of the process as long as the goals are not . . . rammed down your throat. Making sure the teacher has input is one important part of the process that makes it fair.

Providing this input for teachers reinforces teachers' sense of professional autonomy. Coupling evaluation to goal-setting also strengthens the accountability objectives of evaluation. A Mountain View-Los Altos principal, in fact, sees this aspect of evaluation as critical:

> I think maybe the key to the whole process is the coupling we do between the goal setting and the observation-evaluation process. I think the teachers and the public take us more seriously now due to the accountability focus we place on the evaluation system. . . .

Each district has constructed an evaluation system that provides this latitude for teachers. However, the strongest teacher commitment to evaluation appears in districts that join this individual involvement with institutional participation in teacher evaluation. Such commitment is generated not only or even always by mandates that teachers perceive as legitimate, but also by those policies which they believe are in line with their internalized needs (Etzioni, 1975:128). Teacher participation in the development and implementation of an evaluation scheme is the most effective strategy for developing congruence between teachers' values and expectations, organizational goals, and evaluation activities. In addition participation of this nature also promotes the sense of ownership essential to effective implementation and the collegiality that increases general support within the organization (see, for example, Kerr and Slocum, 1981).

SUMMARY

Enabling teacher evaluation begins with the process of unfreezing, of reexamining the understandings, beliefs, and practices fundamental to the institution. Some kind of triggering event appears necessary to turn district personnel from standard operating procedures and sanction significant organizational change. The willingness of teachers and administrators to take up the problem of teacher evaluation in this organizational environment subsequently depended on two factors. One was the presence of activities or factors that legitimized a consequential teacher evaluation system. A second was the express and strong commitment of the superintendent to teacher evaluation. Together these factors focused attention on the problem of teacher evaluation. The trigger, we saw, even if seized by leadership to force basic reconsideration of the organization, is insufficient to persuade people to act on teacher evaluation unless a persuasive rationale for teacher evaluation was also present.

These pressures for evaluation combined with management choices that began to develop the trust and understanding central to consequential evaluation. Open communication throughout the district meant that administrators and teachers felt they were being heard—that the evaluation scheme was not something being sent down upon them. This climate of communication was strengthened in each case by a high level of teacher involvement in developing teaching evaluation. In each district, teachers joined administrators as collaborators in planning for a new evaluation system.

These cases illustrate how efforts to change organizational culture, in this case the culture of evaluation in a district, require first that the old or existing culture be challenged successfully and then that new values and practices replace traditional ones. New teacher evaluation practices cannot simply be grafted on in most districts. Together, the factors we have just described combined to provide an environment that allowed school districts to change the basic norms and expectations that structure behavior—to create a culture of evaluation—so that teacher evaluation could be taken seriously.

Each of the districts we visited were at a somewhat different stage in the process of organizational change associated with establishing this culture or enabling environment. Differences among districts in this respect illustrate the dynamic, iterative quality of organizational change associated with teacher evaluation and highlight the ways in which activities undertaken at the initial stage can be mutually reinforcing.

In Charlotte, career development serves as the focal point of all district policy. In this respect teacher evaluation, as the center of this program, is highly visible and enjoys the commitment of a broad-based group of teachers and administrators. In terms of leadership and organizational strength and stability, Charlotte receives the highest of marks.

Charlotte's efforts to provide for teacher input at all levels of the evaluation process succeeded in fostering open communication throughout the district. The open management style of the superintendent and his crafting of a staged implementation plan over several years laid the groundwork for building trust in the district. Indeed, the office of career development sits just down the hall from superintendent Robinson's office, whose "door is always open" to the new director of career development,

Kay Mitchell. Thus, the necessary set of organizational preconditions for effective teacher evaluation appear to be in place.

In Moraga, Judith Glickman's efforts to make teacher evaluation a priority have succeeded in making it a highly visible issue for teachers and administrators. But several factors combine to depress the levels of trust and communication that are necessary to secure the full commitment of teachers to the evaluation process. Hostility between teachers and the superintendent was so high when Glickman arrived that even the impressive gains she has made with teachers fall short of the degree of trust necessary to successful teacher evaluation. Though no teacher could cite an instance in which their trust in the superintendent's motives and abilities had been betrayed, they remained wary nonetheless, preferring to approach each new district policy cautiously, withholding initial support. Failure to involve teachers more systematically in the initial planning stages coupled with difficulty in securing resources to continue joint teacher-administrator training efforts also combine to lower commitment and inhibit communication. Thus, recent district efforts to encourage teachers to engage in collegial observations and videotaping have met with initial resistance. In sum, the enabling conditions necessary to transform teacher evaluation into a force for teacher improvement are only partially present in Moraga.

Mountain View-Los Altos apparently sits at a critical juncture in the development of an evaluation system that can support teachers' learning. The difficult task of securing trust, open communication, and commitment from teachers and administrators is succeeding only now. Paul Sakamoto's leadership and commitment to teacher evaluation is clear. The strength and stability of the district has enabled it to endure difficult tensions between management and the teachers union. District efforts to bring consistency to evaluation practices have increased teachers' confidence in the process, but in the future, teachers' attitudes may hinge on the manner in which general dissatisfaction regarding the role of the student survey in the evaluation process is resolved. Our interviews suggest that renewed commitment to face-to-face communication and increased teacher involvement in planning the future direction of teacher evaluation must take place in Mountain View-Los Altos to maintain teacher and administrator commitment to district teacher evaluation policy.

Finally, the Santa Clara Unified School District appears to have weathered the turbulent environment of the past several years. Attention is shifting away from maintenance issues of curricular accountability and school reorganization toward an emphasis on instruction. The new Effective Instruction and Support staff-development program and the formation of the district-wide Academy of Excellence (an umbrella for district-wide staff-development efforts) are evidence of this renewed focus on issues of organizational development. Trust is high, and communication channels are in place. However, the lack of attention to evaluation caused by an unsettled environment has eclipsed the visibility of teacher evaluation and has subsequently lowered the commitment of administrators to follow through on the process. Renewed attention on the part of the superintendent may remedy this situation and bring about the necessary commitment for teacher evaluation to be a force for teacher improvement.

While these districts illuminate factors critical to getting started—to enabling teacher evaluation—they also show that building a culture for evaluation is an ongoing, dynamic process. Pressure for evaluation and laying the groundwork for openness and trust through strategies of communication and participation comprise an essential first step. However, these conditions merely enable teacher evaluation to get underway. They do not and cannot ensure the depth and breadth of teacher support required by meaningful evaluation in the long run.

Students of planned change have begun to notice that belief often follows action, that many times doing is believing. For example, teachers initially convinced that low-income parents could offer little useful to their children's education became enthusiastic supporters of significant parent involvement once persuaded to give it a try (McLaughlin and Shields, 1986). Fullan, reviewing curriculum implementation research, concludes, " . . . changes in attitudes, beliefs and understanding tend to *follow* rather than precede changes in behavior" (1986:4).

This developmental perspective suggests two broad conclusions for teacher evaluation. One is that it takes time to establish the norms and culture essential to teacher evaluation.

A second is that the process of building that culture continues well beyond the first stages of getting started. What happens next, or the actual practices of teacher evaluation developed and implemented by the district, plays a critical role in nurturing and strengthening the trust and commitment required just to begin.

CHAPTER 3

Evaluation Processes and Procedures

We found no single recipe or template for teacher evaluation. What works in one district may fall flat in another setting with different organizational traditions, management principles, and governing values or practices. While the goals espoused for teacher evaluation in each district were similar—accountability and improvement—the teacher evaluation efforts we examined differed along all major design parameters—the role of the principal, the role of teachers, the frequency of evaluation, evaluation instrumentation, and institutional responses to evaluation. Further, each district's program defines a different element as the linchpin on which the entire process turns. For example:

- In Charlotte, the success of the system depends on the ability of the advisory/assistance teams to support the teacher through the evaluation process and ultimately to make a summative decision regarding the teacher's status. In addition, the presence of district-wide observer/ evaluators who serve as a mechanism to insure quality control represents a central feature.
- In Moraga, joint training received by teachers and administrators coupled with clinical supervision techniques rests at the heart of the program.
- In Mountain View-Los Altos, multiple sources of information—an evaluation portfolio—including direct observation, samples of student work, results of a student survey, grading distributions, and teacher-made materials—characterize the district's approach to evaluation.
- In Santa Clara, a peer-based remediation process for teachers judged to be at-risk is the system's defining feature. Peers work with teachers for a period of sixty days independently of administrators in an attempt to improve teacher performance or counsel them out of the profession.

These locally appropriate processes are an essential feature of locally supported teacher evaluation systems. The acceptance of teachers and administrators depends in no small measure on the homegrown quality of the plan. This local development allows teacher evaluation strategies to mesh with local management styles and routines (a feature Rand analysts highlighted in their study of successful teacher evaluation [Wise et al., 1984]) and permits local educators to view the system as theirs. Local development is an important component in building and extending trust. However, despite this diversity in overall district plans, several design features emerged across all sites as pivotal in the extent to which teacher evaluation activities achieved the support of teachers and administrators and achieved their objectives. They are

> joint training for administrators and teachers
> systems of checks and balances
> accountability structure for evaluation
> effective feedback procedures
> flexible instrumentation
> integration of evaluation and staff development resources

The districts we visited differed in the extent to which these features characterized their evaluation systems. The consequences associated with the presence or relative absence of each provide important lessons for planners to consider in developing teacher evaluation programs.

JOINT TRAINING
FOR ADMINISTRATORS AND TEACHERS

Few districts can embark successfully on a new teacher evaluation strategy without first investing heavily in additional training for both teachers and administrators. Virtually every recent study of teacher evaluation systems highlights the importance of training in making evaluation work (Bridges, 1986; Stiggins and Bridgeford, 1985; Wise et al., 1984). That research and the experience of the districts included in this book also underscore the importance of shared training targeted to the evaluation process for teachers and administrators. *Joint* training makes important substantive and symbolic contributions to effective teacher evaluation.

The key role of the principal in the outcome of a teacher evaluation effort provides a clear brief for training administrators—jointly or

individually—to improve their evaluation skills. Teachers and administrators in all of the districts we visited emphasized the principal as the
critical link in the evaluation process. Regardless of the formal role of
the principal in a teacher evaluation strategy, he or she is probably the
most important actor (beyond the superintendent) in determining how
well a teacher evaluation plan is carried out in a given school. Rudi Gatti
in Santa Clara spoke for his colleagues in other districts when he said,
"You can have the best teacher evaluation system in the world but if you
don't have principals and administrators committed to it, it just is not
going to fly."

Principals are key to the process for a number of reasons. One is
that principals, by virtue of their institutional role, represent a critical
source of approval for teachers. Our cases show that other evaluators—
peers, departmental supervisors, central-office staff, for example—can provide valuable feedback to teachers, but the involvement of the principal
at some point in the process is critical. A Mountain View-Los Altos teacher
with seven years' experience expressed this well:

> It really made a difference that my evaluator was the principal. After all,
> he hired me and he has trusted all along that I've done a good job. But
> he has never actually gotten into my room and taken a good, hard look.
> So finally when he came in this year and said, "My trust has been well
> placed," that meant a lot to me.

This teacher candidly admitted that the same evaluation received from
one of her other building administrators or from a peer would not have
had as great an impact on her, even though she has great respect for them
and values their views.

Another reason that principals play a key role in any evaluation
system is the signal they send about instructional priorities. How principals spend their time reflects organizational values. Just as principals
take their cue from central-office administrators, teachers look to principals
in establishing priorities. Even in Charlotte-Mecklenburg, where the principal does not play a central role in the evaluation process, we heard strong
statements from teachers regarding the importance of the principal's leadership. For example, one career candidate said:

> If the principal is not involved in the process, teachers in the school probably
> won't see evaluation as being important. How the principal spends his

time sends a powerful message to teachers about the priority that something has in the school. The principal serves as a symbol. If he arranges his schedule to spend time on [evaluation], then teachers get the message.

Practitioners also acknowledge that evaluation generally is not something most principals do easily or well. Respondents in all our districts used the same word to describe the usual principal role in teacher evaluation: "gutless." Principals, like other people, have difficulty delivering "bad news" or negative assessments of an individual performance (Bridges, 1986).

Principals often rationalize this reluctance in terms of a role conflict—conflict between their role as manager and their role as colleague. This is particularly true of principals who have come up through the system. As administrators they are called upon to assess their former colleagues' performance. Training that gives confidence in evaluation skills and reinforces the importance of evaluation to a strong educational program can be an important strategy for imparting evaluator courage. Training for principals, whether they are playing a central or a supportive role, is essential to an effective teacher evaluation system.

However, most administrators and teachers we interviewed stressed the importance of joint training activities for reasons that go beyond mere skill acquisition. Joint training plays a major role in building and sustaining an evaluation culture. For example, Santa Clara Unified School District's superintendent, Rudi Gatti, has actively stressed both the substantive and symbolic features of shared administrator/teacher training. To underscore his view that teacher evaluation is something the *district* takes seriously, Gatti requires central-office administrators to participate in the Effective Instruction and Support program, including teaching a demonstration lesson and receiving coaching. Not only has Gatti completed the training himself, but he has also agreed to be videotaped teaching a lesson to be used as part of future district training efforts. Administrators we interviewed stressed the substantive value of these sessions for them. Teachers pointed to the symbolic value; participation in joint-training activities signaled to teachers that administrators cared enough about evaluation, respected the skills involved, and were committed to evaluation and improvement as tasks for all to work on, not just teachers. Teachers in Santa Clara and in the other districts point to the important function played by joint training in breaking down long-standing barriers between teachers and administrators in schools, barriers that support the distancing and lack of trust that frustrate teacher evaluation.

Joint training also makes another important strategic contribution to teacher evaluation. It provides a common language with which all personnel in the district can discuss instructional practices (Little, 1981). Joint training produces shared capacity because it provides the tools administrators and teachers can use to examine together classroom activities and understand them. A Mountain View-Los Altos vice principal offers an analogy:

> [It is the same problem teachers often have with their students.] Very often as a teacher you'll teach a lesson and think that you've just done a great job. And then you'll give a test and find that only 30% of the students passed. And you'll think to yourself, "Darn. How come they did so badly?" So then you go back and you talk to the students and ask them in different words the same questions that were on the test and then you find out that they actually do know the material. You say to the students, "Why didn't you perform better on the test?" And they'll say, "Because I didn't understand the words you were using" . . . . [It's the same with principals and teachers.]

Shared language also fosters collegiality among participants and allows evaluators to anchor their feedback in shared and specific notions of expert practice. This specificity adds important clarity about expectations and supports an evaluation system in which teachers feel comfortable that there will be no surprises.

In Santa Clara Unified, joint teacher/administrator training occurs in conjunction with the district-wide staff-development program, Effective Instruction and Support. Part of the program involves a teacher's teaching a demonstration lesson and being coached by another individual, often his or her building administrator. Without exception, teachers found the observation and coaching experience in conjunction with the Effective Instruction and Support program much more beneficial to their professional practice than observations that had not been conducted in this context. The shared training provided a framework and a focus for discussion which benefitted both participant and coach. For example, an elementary teacher in Santa Clara said:

> [The participation of teachers and administrators in the Effective Instruction and Support program] has added another dimension to the evaluation process. Evaluations are more clear. They are more fair. I feel I know what I am being evaluated on. It has given me a good feeling and I know now what is expected of me.

A colleague at the high-school level mentioned the symbolic as well as the substantive value of joint training:

> [Joint participation] really made the whole evaluation experience more meaningful for me. Knowing that we both participated [in the Effective Instruction and Support program] made a difference [in how I perceived my evaluator's expertise] . . . because most administrators have been out of the classroom for so long it means a lot to know that your evaluator has had to participate in some kind of actual teaching experience. [It also] gives us some basics that we can both focus on.

Another teacher in Santa Clara underscored this important result of the district's training efforts:

> [Evaluation] definitely has changed for me because of the clinical support program. Rather than come in and make broad, general, and rather meaningless statements—rather than talk about classroom atmosphere, whatever that means—he now talks about specific things that we can both understand. If I ask poor questions, he can explain to me why and suggest ways I can improve my questioning techniques. . . . We provide each other feedback as a result of our involvement [in joint training experiences]. He knows that he does a good job and he's able to tell me that I am doing a good job in specific terms. He can now say things like, "Your class is managed well because . . . " and then follow that with specific suggestions.

The benefits of a shared instructional language between administrators and teachers are readily observable in Moraga, where Glickman has explicitly based the evaluation system in a model of shared training between administrators and teachers. According to one veteran middle-school teacher:

> [Elements of Effective Instruction] brought the teaching staff together, like we used to do a long time ago. . . . It helped strengthen ties. It crossed lines; even the administration was there. It was a cohesive experience that made us feel like a family again. . . . [As a result,] teachers and administrators now talk about instruction at faculty meetings . . . we could all share and talk because we had a common grounding.

Shared training also is important to clarify the rules of the game for all participants. Before any evaluation system can succeed, staff members must fully understand the procedures to be used in arriving at evaluative judgments. As Charlotte's Phillip Schlechty says, "The ideal evaluation system first teaches teachers about the evaluation process." Thus, Charlotte-Mecklenburg requires every staff member, including administrators, to complete an effective teaching workshop.

Mountain View-Los Altos provides an instructive contrast on this point, especially as pressed administrators ask, "How much training is enough? Who should participate?" Mountain View-Los Altos has conducted several training programs for teachers and administrators, but their approach has been less systematic than Charlotte's. The consequences, at this point in the process, are apparent. Participation was voluntary, encouraged by the availability of an incentive pay program. Not every teacher participated in the programs, nor did every administrator. As a result, both teachers and administrators are sometimes unclear regarding the criteria upon which the evaluation will be based and which workshops lie at the core of the evaluation process. Given this uneven exposure, it is not surprising that teachers sometimes perceive that the evaluation process differs considerably depending upon who conducts it.

This lack of clarity about evaluation purposes and processes contributes to nagging doubts among some teachers about the overall fairness of the evaluation system. For example, one Mountain View-Los Altos teacher, who has always received excellent evaluation results, stated that each of her five evaluations, performed by different evaluators, differed considerably along each of the following dimensions: number of observations, timing of observations, goal-setting process, focus of the observations, and use of student survey results. For this teacher and several others in the district, the absence of a common language with which to discuss instruction limits the usefulness of the evaluation process as a professional improvement tool.

Mountain View-Los Altos district-level administrators have identified this concern, however, and a task force of teachers and administrators has submitted an extensive list of criteria that delineate superior and inferior teaching. Current management goals reflect Sakamoto's commitment to providing staff-development training in support of identified district needs. Together, these strategies promise to increase the effectiveness of the evaluation system.

In short, joint training serves as a necessary input to the evaluation process, insuring that individuals possess the knowledge and expertise required to make the system work. It does so because it also supports the development of shared perceptions about evaluation goals, procedures, and common language.

SYSTEMS OF CHECKS AND BALANCES

The evaluation programs we observed all tried to develop a system of checks and balances to promote reliability and validity of the evaluation process as well as its perceived fairness. In each district, the multiple procedures functioned to give teachers a sense of safety—that a bad day or a less-than-perfect performance would not be the sum of an evaluation or result in unreasonable consequences. Without a sense of professional safety, teachers may divert attention away from the experimentation that might improve their performance, focusing instead on maintaining low-risk teaching strategies that meet minimum requirements for success.

Each district uses different strategies to provide checks and balances. In Mountain View-Los Altos, evaluations are based on multiple sources of information, including two or three classroom observations, student surveys, teacher-made materials, student grading distributions, and samples of student work. Every administrator we spoke with described the time-consuming process of gathering together all of the information relevant to a teacher's objectives and then using it to document specific commendations and recommendations. Validity and reliability increase because each piece of information sheds additional and substantively different light on goal attainment by the teacher. As long as no one information source receives heavier weighting than another, teachers perceive the process as fair.

The experience of a department head in Mountain View-Los Altos illustrates the value of this portfolio approach to evaluation. This individual asked a substitute teacher to distribute his student survey forms. All students did not take the exercise seriously, and the teacher received low ratings in several categories. Yet the teacher's response to the appearance of these low ratings on his year-end evaluation demonstrate his trust in the total process. "I don't really get upset because . . . it's not really of any consequence. I know I'm not going to get a bad evaluation as a teacher just because of my student surveys."

In Santa Clara, teachers view the presence of a remediation system as a check on building principals. Since remediation teams are composed of at least two and sometimes three teachers, each one serves as a validator of the others' judgments.

Of the four districts included in this book, Charlotte employs the most sophisticated set of checks and balances. Their strategy reflects Schlechty's commitment to what he calls "the overarching principle of reasonableness." A teacher's advisory/assistance team is composed of three members, one of whom is a peer. Multiple membership forces each individual to hold the others accountable. In addition, observer/evaluators serve as a check to the advisory/assistance team's judgments. Each discrepancy between classroom observations made by observer/evaluators and advisory/assistance team members must be explicitly addressed before a summative judgment can be made about a teacher's performance, and two separate review committees composed of teachers and administrators must validate the findings of each school-based advisory/assistance team regarding a teacher's level of competence. Finally, the superintendent's signature ends the entire review process. This complex system of checks and balances reflects the undergirding principle of the evaluation process in Charlotte-Mecklenburg; multiple evaluations are conducted by numerous individuals employing multiple and explicit criteria over a long period of time.

Statements from individuals at every level of the school district indicate that this notion of professional safety and checks and balances has been effectively communicated even in the early stages of implementation:

> Observer/evaluators serve the need of evaluating the evaluations produced at the school site level. [They serve] as external validators of principal and assistant principal for instruction evaluation reports. . . . They serve a key role. (From a district-level administrator.)

> [The area review committees] are a critical part of the evaluation process because the advisory/assistance teams have to defend the summative judgments they make based on the data in the reports that will be reviewed by the area committee. We give data. We don't evaluate. One of the reasons we have [multiple] observations is to allow for a teacher to have a bad day but the rest of the observations show what their true performance is like. (From an observer/evaluator.)

> The observer/evaluators serve as a check of [teachers'] jobs here at the school. [They] hold us accountable. As API, I read over all the observer/evaluator reports and work with the teachers based on their comments. (From an assistant principal for instruction.)

I think the observer/evaluators are almost unnecessary because the advisory/ assistance team makes the final, ultimate decision. I guess the observer/ evaluator is a check. This is the role it serves. (From a provisional teacher.)

Checks and balances, in short, play a number of important functions. They defuse the "gotcha" quality possible in an evaluation and increase teachers' comfort and thus their openness about their performance. In this way, a system of checks and balances extends and reinforces the trust and confidence necessary to get started with teacher evaluation.

The presence of checks and balances also signals the district's appreciation of the complexity of the teaching task and commitment to undertake evaluation in a serious, professional manner. Finally, a system of checks and balances furnishes overall accountability for the system itself.

ACCOUNTABILITY STRUCTURE FOR EVALUATION

If evaluation is to be taken seriously in the near term, and if it is to be institutionalized in the long term, an accountability structure for evaluation is essential. An evaluation process that supports teacher learning formalizes the dual commitment to expert and formal authority by making it part of a system of accountability that extends from the top to the bottom of the district. We saw that two somewhat different forms of accountability were important to an evaluation system. The first was some kind of system of checks and balances that promotes accountability of the system itself through an emphasis on fairness, professionalism, and expert judgment. The second was accountability for evaluators, holding those who conduct evaluation responsible for their performance in the same way as they hold teachers responsible for theirs.

Accountability for evaluators serves a reinforcing function. Holding evaluators as well as teachers accountable for their performance not only focuses attention—it also reinforces the fact that top leadership sees evaluation as serious business and thus spends time monitoring their activities. Charlotte, again because of its size, has the most elaborate system of accountability, extending into the fabric of the evaluation program itself. The checks and balances serve a dual purpose of insuring a sense of professional safety (described in the previous section), and of holding evaluators accountable for the quality of their evaluations. Advisory/ assistance teams bear the ultimate responsibility for conducting a teacher's evaluation. They not only make the summative judgment regarding the teacher's status, but they also must provide the teacher with all possible assistance in making the grade. When discrepancies between observer/ evaluator and advisory/assistance team reports arise, the advisory/assistance team must decide if unique, extenuating circumstances caused the divergence, or if they have been remiss in managing the evaluation process. The following comment from an area superintendent indicates that such occurrences will not be taken lightly:

> If there are differences, then we can probe them more deeply to see if there is a need for us [the district office] to provide some assistance. I don't let them [advisory/assistance teams] off the hook. I insist that they arrive at a decision that they can justify . . . . They must make the final decision. All we want to do is review it.

This accountability structure insures that the evaluation system functions as planned.

The small size of Moraga and Mountain View-Los Altos makes administrative accountability for evaluation results a simpler process. Central-office administrators, including the superintendent in both districts, read the evaluations and observations reports of teachers prepared by administrators and critique their quality. Administrators are explicitly evaluated on the quality of these evaluation reports. In Mountain View-Los Altos, skill as an evaluator represented a major criterion used in selecting a new principal for one of the high schools. Principals in Mountain View-Los Altos are clear about expectations for their performance as evaluators:

> Because of the demands parents make in this system, the evaluation system is under a lot of pressure. And this is focused all the way down through the system. My bosses look at the evaluations I write; we actually discuss these evaluations sometimes in our management meetings. So accountability filters all the way down through the system from the superintendent down to the teachers.

The positive effects of holding evaluators accountable for evaluation results is best illustrated in Santa Clara. When the remediation program was first introduced eight years ago, principals did not refer any teachers during the first year. Yet Gatti knew that incompetent teachers existed in the system. Thus, he and his line administrators placed several building principals on remediation for their failure to execute their evaluative responsibilities. Not surprisingly, eight teachers were placed on remediation the following year.

But as we have already discussed, Gatti's attention to the evaluation system has been diverted in recent years, and this has been accompanied by a lack of administrative accountability for evaluation results—lack of attention on the part of principals to teacher evaluation. Administrators receive little feedback on their evaluations of teachers. Those in the central office charged with responsibility for evaluating principals do not routinely view teacher evaluation reports prepared by principals. As one central-office administrator put it, "I suppose we should get copies of the evaluations here, but we dont, so we have to rely on [the personnel director]. This may be a weak point in our process." Insuring that the quantity of evaluations completed by administrators meets minimal expectations takes priority over their quality. As one result, teacher evaluation is conducted somewhat unevenly throughout the district.

An accountability structure for teacher evaluation, in summary, serves important functions as a strategy for focusing administrators' attention on teacher evaluation and as a way to keep channels of communication about evaluation open and active. The more principals and district administrators discuss teacher evaluation activities, the more expectations can be clarified, the more impediments to strong evaluation can be identified and addressed. But, as the districts we visited show, accountability for teacher evaluation has to begin at the top, with the superintendent.

EFFECTIVE FEEDBACK PROCEDURES

Feedback, the process of giving back information for the purpose of bringing about change in the behavior of those receiving the information, sits at the heart of any teacher evaluation effort. Teacher evaluation potentially is such a powerful feedback mechanism because evaluation is a way of *giving* meaning to activity. But it can play this important role only if it is received, if it is heard, and if it is acted upon. As the experiences of most school districts testify, feedback associated with most teacher evaluation activities typically does not serve this purpose and so can promote neither improvement nor accountability.

What is effective feedback? The teacher evaluation activities we observed join with the general literature on organizational behavior to suggest that effective feedback must have the following characteristics:

timeliness
specificity
credibility
intent (perceived as nonpunitive)

Timeliness

Timeliness is important because motivation to change as well as anxiety about outcomes are highest immediately following an evaluation session. Feedback provided immediately after a classroom observation—when events are fresh in the minds of both teacher and evaluator—has maximum learning potential. Follow-up that comes weeks or months later is too late to be of any use.

But to be effective, feedback must also be geared to the rhythms of the classroom. Feedback at year's end loses its impact when summer vacation intervenes. The timing of feedback in Mountain View-Los Altos illustrates the problems associated with a typical evaluation format. Though the multiple sources of information that evaluators employ in preparing a teacher's evaluation report provide rich, descriptive data regarding a teacher's performance, its usefulness to the teacher for professional growth purposes is limited because it is presented at the end of the year just prior to summer recess. Since teachers are evaluated only every other year, most of our respondents reported that they rarely attended to results of their evaluations until just prior to the following evaluation cycle. The notable exceptions to this were those individuals who were rated as unsatisfactory— they remained on a yearly evaluation cycle until acceptable performance emerged.

Specificity

Specificity is important to effective feedback in all organizations (see, for example, Argyris, 1982; Kerr and Slocum, 1981); it is especially critical in education where teachers, as clinically based professionals, judge their effectiveness primarily in terms of student responses (Lortie, 1975; McLaughlin, Pfeifer, Swanson-Owens, and Yee, 1986). Generalities or theoretical abstractions have little meaning for teachers as assessments of their performance or as a guide for growth. The comments of this Charlotte teacher capture of teachers' views on this point:

> [Before the new evaluation system was implemented], all I got were these check in the "excellent" column of my year-end evaluation with comments such as "excellent teacher." The problem was that there was never any help for my professional growth. I'm a teacher with seventeen years' experience and I knew I was good, but the lack of feedback was really distressing. Later on in my career it was just too easy to sit back on my laurels and accept where I was and not try to improve anymore. Let's face it, there is always room for growth no matter where you are or how good you are . . . [this new process gives me the information I need to do that.]

Specificity also is critical because it enables the evaluator to engage the evaluatee in assessment of evidence. Whereas interpretations may be disputed, data closely tied to the observation or event allow individuals to draw their own conclusions. And where disagreement occurs, evaluators and teachers can refer to what actually occurred and interpret it together. In this way the specificity of evaluative feedback encourages open, constructive confrontation and can defuse the defensiveness that often makes teachers unwilling to hear an evaluator's comments. One administrator in Mountain View-Los Altos found that preparing a draft of a teacher's final evaluation report as a basis for discussion was particularly beneficial in this regard. With concrete evidence as the basis, she never failed to engage the teacher in a way that both find worthwhile. Presenting material in draft form minimized defensive behavior and allowed evaluator and evaluatee to match interpretations and perceptions of the evidence at hand.

Specificity of feedback also signals that the evaluator has taken evaluation seriously. In fact, teachers find general, apparently casual evaluation insulting. The comments of a teacher in Santa Clara were echoed by teachers in each district who had experienced superficial evaluation:

> I had only one observation [this year], but I never had a chance to sit down with my evaluator and look at what he wrote. This year he just caught me in the hall and said, "I'm going to drop by and see you sometime this week." Then two weeks later he dropped into my class unannounced . . . several days later he stopped me in the hall and said, "You had a great observation." To be honest, I felt somewhat brushed off. In fact, I was downright offended because when you evaluate someone that way, you're

basically talking about the dignity and worth of the individual. If evaluation is going to have any meaning, there's a need to have more face-to-face contact. After all, I probably have areas where I'm not really as effective as I could be, and there are things that I'm doing in my classes that I must may not be aware of. I really missed not having any professional exchange with someone who was trying to look for those things . . . after all, it's very hard to be an effective self-evaluator . . . I really missed the feedback from not being evaluated carefully this year and I also felt offended.

Charlotte provides teachers in the Career Development Program extensive feedback—provisional teachers may receive as many as forty classroom observations and follow-up conferences in a single year. Mentors, assistant principals for instruction, the principal, observer/evaluators, and area program specialists are all involved in providing feedback throughout the year. Both the quantity and quality of the feedback provisional teachers receive accelerates their maturation as effective teachers. One principal estimated that his provisional teachers displayed the characteristics of "three-year veterans" at the end of only one year of participation in the Career Development Program.

Career candidates, however, are assumed to be proficient in classroom pedagogy, and the evaluation process extends to other aspects of teachers' professional life as identified in their Action Growth Plan. Observer/evaluators conduct nine classroom observations, both announced and unannounced, to verify the competence of the candidate's classroom performance, while the advisory/assistance team assists the teacher in completing the Action Growth Plan. Periodic meetings of advisory/assistance teams with the career candidate provide an opportunity to discuss progress in achieving goals set by the teacher. In this manner, credible feedback is linked to a support structure designed to foster growth.

Credibility

Credibility is a central and obvious feature of an effective feedback strategy; feedback that is not seen as credible, reliable, or valid is dismissed out of hand. For an individual to recognize a problem or acknowledge a needed change, he or she must first perceive that feedback comes from a respected source with legitimate claims to expertise.

An effective feedback system, then, must be characterized by expertise-based authority. Teachers must respect the judgment of their evaluators in order to act on their diagnoses for performance or prescriptions for change. Even positive comments are meaningless and ill-received if a teacher perceives an evaluator as lacking substantive expertise. As one Santa Clara teacher illustrates:

> There was never much trust I had in his competence. I never paid much attention to what he said about anything in my instruction. Most of the time he made very broad statements like, "She did an effective job," things that really don't have much meaning. . . . Teachers get very upset when they are evaluated [by my principal]. In fact, even when he said positive things, they told me that it was an insult to their intelligence because he didn't have any skills at all. He didn't know beans about classroom instruction so the pat on the back he gave them was just an insult.

Intent

The most critical feature of effective feedback involves teachers' perceptions of its intent. Any evaluative situation where important consequences hang in the balance will produce anxiety for those involved. If teachers perceive evaluation to be punitive, then the value of concrete feedback might have become lost in an effort to subvert the system and hide shortcomings. A Mountain View-Los Altos teacher with ten years of experience who has always received excellent evaluations described the negative effects of an evaluation system that teachers perceive as punitive:

> [Evaluation] is something that they [the administration] use to try to get rid of people that they don't like. It's not focused on instruction and it's a waste of teachers' time . . . I believe that instruction suffers because we as teachers get tense and nervous and waste time polishing up apples for the administrators when we could be spending that time more productively preparing our lessons.

When teachers rightly or wrongly perceive evaluation to be punitive, they exhibit a rational and adaptive response: In an attempt to find safety and protection, they become defensive, try to hide errors, and minimize risk-taking. Ironically, evaluation perceived as punitive can actually generate incompetence in the course of trying to prevent it. Being candid and up-front about an individual's performance without the evaluators' appearing that they are "out to get" the teacher requires a delicate balancing act.

Good intentions are not enough; teachers must believe that they will be supported in their change efforts, with success the ultimate goal.

Teacher reactions to evaluation in Mountain View-Los Altos illustrate both the critical importance of perceived emphasis and the value of credible, specific feedback. Year-end evaluation reports range from four single-spaced pages of narrative documentation for teachers rated satisfactory, to over twenty pages for someone rated unsatisfactory. We spoke with teachers in both categories who found the care and precision with which their evaluator documented their teaching to be valuable. For example, one teacher rated highly effective by one administrator described her evaluation this way:

> [My evaluator] wrote careful pages and pages of detailed observations and data. He not only talked about the student survey, he analyzed it. He looked at test results and analyzed them from my language class and also looked at the test results from my AP class. . . . He quoted in his report things that I and my students said in an effort to document my effectiveness. He examined class materials that I produced and student products— notebooks that they made. . . . And he wrote this all up with great [sensitivity] . . . .

But some Mountain View-Los Altos teachers see evaluative feedback as a punitive device rather than an occasion for reflection and growth, and these perceptions appear to have a basis in fact. According to one Mountain View-Los Altos administrator, grievances filed in reference to evaluation procedures have been a driving force in recent changes in the evaluation process. As a result, the teacher evaluation system has taken on a "legalistic" focus during that time. Several administrators specifically mentioned the legalistic focus of recent summer workshops. Another administrator felt that this focus partially explained the negative attitude toward evaluation, which had been particularly acute the previous year:

> The focus [of evaluation] is on documenting things that stand up in court rather than letting teachers know what kind of job they are doing. . . . In fact, we were told by one legal consultant to be very careful about using positive comments because this can have an adverse effect in a court case and actually be used against us. . . . This legalistic approach to evaluation has rubbed off. It's created a very negative morale situation in the district.

As one teacher put it, "[Evaluation] is almost an adversarial situation." Another veteran male teacher who has always received excellent evaluations from his principal described the deleterious effects when the perceived emphasis of the evaluation process shifts toward a rule-driven system:

> Most important of all is that evaluations be approached on a level such as, "I am here not to put you down but to see how well you are doing. Not just to implement the contract but to see if there is anything you can do for yourself through a process of self-awareness that will help you improve in the classroom. I'm not here to be a threat." If evaluation techniques take place within this context, not only will it be fair, but it will also be useful. Unfortunately this has not been the case with teachers in the district [and evaluations lose any value they might have].

Some Mountain View-Los Altos administrators feel very constrained by the standardized, legal framework within which evaluations must be cast, reducing their ability to affect teacher growth in a positive manner. Though these measures have increased the likelihood that evaluation results will stand up in an administrative hearing, they also function to depress risk-taking and "public" response to evaluation outcomes. Superintendent Sakamoto admits that "We've had several attorneys as consultants and I would admit that they may have had a greater impact than they should."

Recent movement away from a punitive, legalistic focus for teacher evaluation in Mountain View-Los Altos is noted by teachers, however. We interviewed several teachers who approached their coming evaluations with trepidation, only to be reassured by the fair and totally thorough procedure that ensued. Having experienced the benefits of evaluation first-hand, their trust in the positive orientation of the process has strengthened.

Superintendent Sakamoto, along with several building administrators, believes that much of the apprehension experienced by teachers stems from the necessity to "start somewhere." Any time performance standards rise, anxiety increases. But administrators in the district are aware of the need to manage teacher perceptions regarding the focus of evaluative feedback. The fact that 95% of the teachers in the district recently indicated that their most recent evaluation was fair and objective indicates that a turnaround is occurring. According to one building administrator:

> Bringing consistency to the [evaluation] process is something that we may be able to do a better job on. There are just lots of things that we have to deal with. But teachers are correct in their complaints—we do expect a lot more of them now than we did five years ago. And so the root of the problems we are experiencing in teacher satisfaction has to do with the fact that we started midstream.

According to the president of the local teachers' association:

> I don't think there are any major problems [with evaluation]. I think things have changed over the years and evolved. We have less complaints about evaluation this year than we did last year, so hopefully things are improving.

Within Charlotte's Career Development Program, we also encountered individuals who perceived the evaluation process to be punitive. Not surprisingly, in every instance, their advisory/assistance teams had failed to support them. In some cases they had failed to meet on a regular basis; in others, team members failed to understand the role they were expected to play. In either case, the teachers involved found evaluation to be a negative experience and the feedback they received useless.

In summary, the nature of feedback associated with teacher evaluation practices has an obvious and central role in determining the outcomes of teacher evaluation. Timing, specificity, credibility, and intent are critical to the effectiveness of feedback. These factors establish the value of evaluation for teachers and consequently their commitment to it. The responses of teachers in the districts we studied show that "more is more"— that the more teachers perceive evaluation feedback as helpful and as an aid to their professional development, the more they are willing to support strong evaluation and to engage in the effectively public experimentation and risk-taking important to learning new skills. Even teachers previously skeptical about the worth of evaluation became advocates as a result of feedback they thought was accurate and beneficial. Two additional design features, we found, were important to teachers' judgments about the quality of the feedback they received—flexible instruments and evaluation-linked resources.

FLEXIBLE INSTRUMENTATION

The districts we observed used two kinds of evaluation instruments: open-ended strategies and the more traditional checklists. The instruments both teachers and administrator/evaluators found most useful were flexible and allowed evaluators to tailor comments to the specifics of a teacher's classroom. In fact, the evaluation instrument favored in all four districts was a blank page. Evaluators recorded activities and teacher behaviors as they occurred and used the resulting classroom specific documentation to assess a teacher's performance, to point to areas of strength and weakness, and to illustrate patterns in classroom activities.

But a blank page does not signal absence of structure. In each district, the structure for evaluation is provided by two sources: the goals teachers established for themselves at the beginning of the year and the instructional percepts conveyed in the district's training activities for administrators and teachers. As a result, the evaluation was driven not by the evaluation tool but by the teacher's personal goals and by the specifics of the classroom.

Each district moved toward this open-ended style of evaluation because they felt that standardized checklists were unable to capture the nuances and complexities of the teaching task. Evaluators in each district reported that only open-ended instrumentation of this sort could provide the concrete, situation-specific information necessary to effective feedback.

Similarly, evaluators in all districts reported dissatisfaction and problems with the standardized instrumentation included in their evaluation program. For example, a Moraga administrator called the district's year-end form, a checklist with more than twenty-five items, a "dinosaur." In Moraga, as in other districts we visited, principals respond to the forced-choice assessments with inflated ratings, which undermine the entire process. Moraga plans to eliminate the form at the end of a review process, but its inflexibility is cited by teachers and administrators as a major problem with the current evaluation system.

Likewise in Santa Clara Unified School District, the year-end evaluation form requires the evaluator to make a summative rating of the teacher—"meets district standards," "needs improvement," or "remediation required." Recently, the district modified the summative checklists in an effort to curb inflationary ratings. The evaluation committee removed an "outstanding" category from the form in response to complaints by administrators and teachers that it generated problems. Yet the first year of the new revised form produced just as many complaints from teachers who felt that their performances was not being adequately recognized.

In all districts, administrators find summary categories constraining— focusing on the summative rating removes attention from the documentation of strengths and weaknesses. And teachers find little motivation in such a scheme. One veteran teacher commented, "It's just not necessary to do this 'unsatisfactory' stuff to force a person to improve." It was evident that the lists that appear in policy manuals primarily serve bureaucratic purposes of due process but have little meaning for teachers. For example, though the year-end evaluation form in both Moraga and Santa Clara Unified School Districts contains lists of over twenty-five specific teaching expectations, none of the teachers we interviewed could name more than one or two of them.

Yet some kind of standardized instrumentation is necessary to join the dual evaluation goals of accountability and improvement. Charlotte and Mountain View-Los Altos appear to have come closest to a solution of developing instrumentation that could serve both formative and summative purposes. Their year-end instruments provide a summative assessment of teachers' performance, as does the year-end instrument in other districts. But instead of standardized checklists, they have developed forms that require detailed, narrative statements about a teacher's performance on specific teaching competencies identified by the district, stressed in training activities, and integrated with the teacher's individual goals and objectives.

However, the importance of flexibility does not mean lack of structure or clarity. Teachers and administrators commented on the importance of a high degree of *formalization* and *consistency* in the evaluation system. Formalization was reflected in the evaluation process and evaluation objectives, while permitting evaluators flexibility in identifying the issues and emphases specific to each evaluation.

In every district, evaluator training activities focused on skills that increased inter-evaluator reliability. Each summer in Mountain View-Los Altos, for example, administrators actually sit down and critique evaluation reports prepared the previous year. As an evaluation strategy, then, flexibility must coexist with consistency. While the value of flexible instruments lies in the ability of evaluators to tailor their comments to a particular teacher and a particular classroom, evaluation outcomes that appear to vary with the identity of the evaluator quickly lose credibility, rendering evaluative feedback useless.

INTEGRATION OF EVALUATION
AND STAFF–DEVELOPMENT RESOURCES

Integration of district-wide staff-development resources and the evaluation process constitutes a final important design feature we saw to be central to teachers' receptivity to an evaluation system and belief in its value. In many school districts, staff development remains isolated within the organization and seldom is tied to evaluation activities. Development efforts often lack a consistent focus, ultimately becoming fragmented and uncoordinated (Hyde and Moore, 1982). In contrast, the districts studied attempted to focus all management activities on organizational goals that highlight individual improvement. Staff development, therefore, is a high district priority. According to the assistant superintendent for personnel in Charlotte-Mecklenburg,

> You can't separate individual development from organizational goals. . . . We expect teachers to perform [according to system-wide goals], but we not only expect them to, we train them so they are able to do it. Teachers are evaluated on the way they present material. This is how the two systems [staff development and evaluation] are linked.

We have already discussed the role that staff development plays as *input* to the evaluation process. Development resources play an even more important role in support of evaluation *outputs*. Without training resources to support evaluative feedback, neither evaluator nor evaluatee are motivated to invest time and energy in the evaluation process. Not surprisingly, without the support of development resources targeted to the feedback they receive, teachers see evaluation as a no-win situation in which problems are identified but tools with which to address them are not provided. An effective evaluation system enables teachers not only to identify a problem but also to act to solve it.

Resources also are important to an evaluator's perception about the task of evaluation. We found that evaluators are less likely to provide honest, critical assessments of teachers' expertise unless they know they can ultimately support improvement efforts with resources at their disposal. Without resources to assist a teacher in their improvement efforts, evaluators see themselves as "playing God" or as providing empty critique, a role few managers enjoy.

Integration of development resources and teacher evaluation requires a shift in the way many school districts define staff development. Most administrators, when asked about their district's staff-development efforts, will point to programs and workshops—often one-shot treatments targeted to a particular district problem. But if teacher evaluation is to serve as a source of teacher learning, staff-development resources need to be conceived in much broader terms. Fellow teachers, community resources, district workshops, professional conferences—any and all of these resources exist to support professional growth in any district. However, schools rarely assist teachers in identifying domains for future professional growth in light of organizational needs, nor do they match these needs with available resources and provide the time and incentive for teachers to pursue them. Staff development, conceived in this fashion and linked to the evaluation process, redefines the role of the evaluator from an inspector to a manager of opportunities for professional growth based on evaluative feedback.

Charlotte tightly relates evaluative results to district development resources. The main purpose of the advisory/assistance team is to serve as a broker of staff-development resources in support of the teacher. Through the evaluation system, new ideas, new methods, and enthusiasm are being generated which are then channeled back into district improvement efforts. As Charlotte's Phillip Schlechty states, "What we need to do is to make the good teachers resources for the ones that have difficulty in given situations." Thus, in one school, based on the results of first semester evaluation reports, the district staff-development office planned five school-site workshops to support career candidates here.

The assistant principal for instruction (API) in each of Charlotte-Mecklenburg's schools plays a critical role as the broker of district staff-development resources. His or her actions in each building determine the quality of the support a teacher receives in responding to evaluative feedback. APIs meet periodically to discuss their concerns and share resources and ideas they might bring to bear to support evaluative feedback. Their formal role in the evaluation process has enabled them to expand on the support services they prescribe for teachers, because their knowledge of specific needs is more complete. For example, one API in a high school stated:

> We have provided specific assistance [to provisional teachers] such as assertive discipline workshops and I'm not sure that some of these teachers would have been referred to them without having this evaluation system in place. For example, last year I didn't refer anyone to specific workshops in the district. This year, I've done it at least five times.

The remediation process in Santa Clara Unified School District illustrates very clearly the value of placing training resources at the disposal of evaluators. Remediation specialists have a virtual free hand to utilize any resource to support the improvement of the teacher they are supervising. Remediation team members allow the teacher to obtain release time to observe other successful teachers. They refer the teacher to workshops offered by the district and the state education office. They recommend university courses or courses such as the Bay Area Writing Project or assertive discipline workshops to the teacher, which the school system will pay for. According to one remediation specialist, "I got a blank check agreement that I could use all the substitute time I wanted and that the teacher could have a substitute if she wanted to observe us." Because of this support, all the remediation team members we talked with agreed that teachers unable to improve should not be responsible for students in the classroom.

Mountain View-Los Altos couples their staff-development program even more tightly as an output with the evaluation process. The current series of staff-development workshops arose from careful inspection of the previous year's year-end evaluation reports for teachers. Topics such as "teaching for higher-order-thinking skills" and "classroom management techniques" assist teachers in implementing the recommendations of their evaluators. According to one veteran teacher:

> There is no doubt in my mind that evaluation does help teachers improve. The workshops, the suggestions from the principal, the materials they make available to you—all of these are good. . . . There is certainly lots of assistance in this district for improvement . . . it is sort of hand and glove. They provide you help and then they evaluate you on what you have learned.

Linking staff development to evaluative feedback in this manner helps teachers to maintain existing performance expectations and increases the likelihood that they will attempt to improve. One necessary step in both accountability and improvement is for teachers to recognize a problem. The next critical step is for them to be able to identify a response—to act on the feedback provided through evaluation. Resources tied to evaluation are a necessary part of that problem-solving activity.

SUMMARY

For most school districts, teacher evaluation will require fundamental change in the values and practices that characterize the organization. A necessary set of enabling conditions—a triggering event, environmental stability, leadership committed to strong teacher evaluation together with active teacher involvement in the design and implementation of a teacher evaluation effort—combine to produce an environment of visibility for evaluation, trust, communication, and commitment. Without these organizational conditions, there is little chance that teacher evaluation can become a force for positive individual or institutional change because long-standing norms governing teacher and administrator interaction in schools will thwart it. An initial climate of support for evaluation is necessary to the success of any teacher evaluation scheme.

But in the presence of these enabling conditions, we see how program design considerations function to reinforce and to sustain teachers' and administrators' support for evaluation. Developing and sustaining a culture for teacher evaluation demands program design choices that sustain trust and open communication between teachers and administrators and that lead to outcomes held to be of value by all participants.

Teacher evaluation strategies that are based in joint training of administrators and teachers provide common language and shared expectations and so are important to fostering openness and trust. A system of checks and balances amplifies this sense of trust for teachers because teachers feel that multiple sources and multiple perspectives contribute to a fair, comprehensive assessment. A system of checks and balances also acknowledges the assumptions of professionalism inherent in the system and testifies to the district's commitment to evaluation.

An accountability structure for evaluation serves similar purposes. In addition, it focuses administrators' attention on the quality of the evaluation process and thus contributes the continuing pressure necessary to a vital evaluation system. Effective feedback, which relies on flexible instrumentation and evaluation-based resources, is essential to a strong evaluation culture and to the continued support of participants because it determines the ultimate value of evaluation for participants. Did something result from the process that provided insight into classroom practices? That pointed to promising ways of approaching a problem? That illuminated a "blind side"? Teachers and principals respond positively to a process that helps them to do their jobs better and to grow professionally. The teacher evaluation processes we observed, albeit to varying degrees, were perceived by administrators and teachers as compatible with the broad goals of educating youngsters and with notions of professionalism. Thus these evaluation systems also functioned to serve the broad goals of accountability and improvement.

The next chapter discusses in greater detail the multiple outcomes associated with teacher evaluation practices having these characteristics.

CHAPTER 4

Moving Toward
Accountability and Improvement

"Accountability" and "improvement" figure prominently in every educator's vocabulary and in the objectives adopted for state and local reform initiatives. The way these terms are used implies agreement and clearly understood implications for practice. However, the experiences examined in this book warn that this is not the case. We see that *how* these objectives are conceived matters critically to launching and to sustaining a teacher evaluation effort. Usual conceptions of accountability and improvement are inadequate guides to practice and are, in fact, often counterproductive. Getting started with teacher evaluation means rethinking what accountability and improvement mean in policy and in practice.

Each of the districts we studied adopted accountability and improvement as the broad goals for their teacher evaluation system. Each has moved toward these goals in varying degrees. But as important as their differential success, per se, their experiences highlight the problems that result from facile or unexamined conceptions of accountability and improvement. The cases we studied suggest how limited traditional conceptions set the stage for the disappointing outcomes associated with most teacher evaluation efforts.

In most state and local policy settings, accountability has come to be seen as quality control from the top and to be defined in terms of minimal competencies. A district is thought to be "accountable" if it is using teacher evaluation to identify and to eliminate teacher incompetence. However, the experience of the districts we studied underscores the fact that accountability is and must be more than inspection for minimal performance.

Accountability, these districts remind us, means *to render an account* of individual and institutional performance. Thus accountability means more than giving bad grades for inadequate performance. It means marking competent and excellent performance as well. Evidence generated by the four districts included here demonstrate that teachers want and require accountability of this comprehensive sort. Moreover, these cases show that the ability of a teacher evaluation system to meet accountability goals in a minimalist sense depends importantly on the extent to which good performance is acknowledged as well.

The experience we observed also shows the importance of rethinking the traditional notions of improvement associated with teacher evaluation. Improvement typically has been taken to mean remediation—improving the skills of teachers whose performance is judged below par in some respect. The districts in this book demonstrate that, like accountability, notions of improvement must be extended to all teachers if the evaluation system as a whole is to be seen as legitimate. Teacher evaluation that frames improvement only in terms of the incompetent teacher, or less-than-satisfactory performance, like an accountability objective framed in minimalist terms, is viewed as punitive and inconsistent with professional values. It also is viewed as irrelevant by most teachers in the district, who collect pro forma "satisfactory" marks, and as unrewarding inspection by evaluators.

The experience of the districts we studied also suggest that improvement is a complex, multifaceted notion. Individual improvement has at least two components: (1) *reflection* about teaching and areas of strength and weakness and (2) *motivation* to change or to act on the results of reflection.

But if individual improvement is to result in institutional improvement, individual goals and development efforts must have a third characteristic: a high level of *integration* with district goals and priorities. District plans, then, must acknowledge these three aspects of improvement if improvement is to occur at the institutional level.

How do these themes express themselves in practice? Evidence from the four districts provides rich and concrete illustration of the importance of conceptions of accountability and improvement and of the individual and institutional benefits associated with teacher evaluation.

ACCOUNTABILITY

At the least, effective teacher evaluation systems must provide quality control at the institutional and individual level (Bridges, 1986). Accountability for minimum acceptable performance levels is a stated and important goal of virtually every teacher evaluation system (Wise et al., 1984; Educational Research Service, 1978).

Accountability operates at both the individual and the institutional level. At the individual level, objective feedback provides teachers with accounts of their work which they can compare to their own personal standards. Regardless of a teacher's competence level, specific, concrete, and credible information serves this purpose. At the institutional level, evaluation matches professional performance and district standards, thereby making the institution accountable to its constituency.

A somewhat surprising finding of this study, given vocal teachers' concerns about evaluation processes and procedures and public cynicism about accountability in education, is the high level of teacher support for strong evaluation-based accountability procedures. (Our finding is consistent with Bridges, 1986, and with the case studies contained in Wise et al., 1984.) For example, a Moraga teacher said, "I wouldn't like it [if there were no evaluation] . . . I'd feel that [administrators] did not care enough to check and make sure things are right . . . it is management's responsibility to make sure. I want some accountability." A Mountain View-Los Altos department coordinator asserts that

> The view that teachers are "professionals" and shouldn't be subject to administrators who inspect and evaluate what they do is [hogwash]. We need people to come in and check on us just like anybody else. As long as it is done in a positive and constructive manner, all it can do is benefit education.

A teacher in Santa Clara commented:

> A person shouldn't be given responsibility to take care of kids in a teaching responsibility if they can't teach. The others of us work too hard. If you can't cut it, you should get out of the profession.

A Santa Clara administrator reinforces this view but from a somewhat different perspective. He notes that ineffective teachers often are glad to hear specific comments about areas of weak performance:

> It's tough to give people negative evaluations, but I'm amazed, actually. I've actually given more "needs improvement" in the last four years than any time before . . . I'm amazed that once I put everything on the table, teachers are often relieved that someone has finally told them in a candid manner what they think of their teaching.

Although popular notions of teachers and accountability run counter to these views, they are not at all surprising when viewed in light of the incentives and rewards that characterize the teaching profession. For most teachers, a desire to serve students lies at the base of professional incentives. Ineffective classroom performance, whatever the cause, robs teachers of the rewards that drew them to the classroom in the first place. Few incompetent teachers enjoy their jobs. Yet in the absence of evaluation and careful documentation, teachers often rationalize their poor performance, usually blaming the students for their failure. For example, remediation specialists in the Santa Clara Unified School District described their first observation of a poorly performing teacher in just this manner. At the end of a disastrous lesson, the teacher's initial comment was, "See how bad those kids are?"

Teacher evaluation promotes individual accountability by forcing teachers to confront objective accounts of their own teaching practice. Careful, detailed, and formal documentation of classroom events can make what is invisible to the teacher visible. We found that when coupled with resources to assist them in improvement efforts, teachers usually seek ways to improve and feel positively about the challenge. As the teacher who had just recently completed a year of remediation in Mountain View-Los Altos commented,

> I'm really excited about getting a fresh start next year. I really believe I have to [make changes in my teaching behavior], if only for my own happiness.

One teacher likened the teacher evaluation process to an accountability system familiar to all teachers—grading students:

> There are some students that you can give a low grade to and they will accept this if they perceive the total process as fair and equitable. Well the same is true with the evaluation of teachers. If the process is perceived as fair and accurate and is treated as a matter of fact and not in a personal way, and everything is clear and up front, then if a person gets a less than satisfactory evaluation, this can be okay.

We also found that the same norms and values that lead teachers to improve on the basis of evaluation feedback also lead teachers to resign voluntarily when fair, credible evidence suggests that they are not well-suited to teaching. Among the three California districts we visited, none has been forced to institute formal dismissal proceedings for incompetence against any tenured teacher. However, each district has secured voluntary resignations from several teachers in conjunction with the evaluation process.

This individual response to evaluation evidence translates into accountability for a minimal level of teacher performance at the institutional level. For example, in Moraga, Glickman estimates that more than 10% of the district's teachers have resigned over the past four years on the basis of evaluation evidence that showed them to be ineffective. The personal interviews she held each year with her professional staff revealed important career goals for each individual. Without exception, the poorly performing teachers were unhappy in their current position, yet economic pressures prevented them from giving up their teaching position and maintaining a comparable standard of living. The district was able to craft an individual package involving early retirement, career counseling, and benefit packages for individuals who secured their resignation, which, according to Glickman and other district respondents, enabled them to leave with positive attitudes.

In Mountain View-Los Altos over the past eight years, ten teachers, approximately 3% of the teaching force, have been induced to resign in a manner similar to Moraga. Approximately 4% of the district's teachers receive an unsatisfactory rating in any given year. Many of these individuals improve to a satisfactory level in the following year.

In the Santa Clara Unified School District, assistant superintendent of personnel Nicholas Gervasse reports that twenty-four teachers have been referred for formal remediation within the district over the past eight years, with one-half of them voluntarily resigning either during or at the end of the process. In addition, approximately twelve other teachers have chosen to resign rather than participate in the remediation process. In each case, Gervasse stated that he attempts to secure a voluntary resignation in lieu of a formal dismissal so that both parties come out a winner. According to Gervasse, the strength of the remediation process is the detailed documentation it produces regarding a teacher's performance that is coupled with intensive assistance from knowledgeable peers.

In Charlotte, institutional-level accountability is revealed in a slightly different manner than the California districts. Provisional teachers require anywhere from three to seven years to obtain tenure, which comes with the attainment of Career Level I status. Eighty-six of the district's 350 provisional teachers have voluntarily resigned, in part due to the extensive feedback generated by the evaluation system. Some decided that teaching was not the career they wished to pursue. Others moved out of the area. Charlotte's director of career development estimates that 6% of the provisional teachers were induced to resign as a direct result of negative evaluative feedback. However, the new evaluation system must be operative for several years before more complete statistics will be generated to compare the current evaluation system to past practices.

The 150 career candidates voluntarily participating in the Career Development Program in its first year were nominated by their supervisors and peers as exemplary teachers (one of several conditions for participation in the first year). Thirteen of these individuals did not attain Career Level I status. Five voluntarily dropped out of the program during the school year, and six voluntarily agreed to extend their status as career candidates for a second year before going through the formal review process. Two individuals were denied Career Level I status at the end of the formal review process. Maintaining high performance standards remains a central goal of the Career Development Program, and these initial results seem to indicate progress in this direction.

In summary, our data reinforce the notion that commitment to professional standards and norms can serve as a powerful source of organizational control. Teacher evaluation that produces information consistent with professional values—what we have called effective feedback—supports accountability of the most fundamental kind because it works through the system's *normative* structures rather than through rule-based bureaucratic procedures.

But our districts caution us that accounting and accountability must mean more than giving and responding to bad grades. Good grades are a necessary and usually overlooked aspect of an accountability effort. Accountability is not reserved for the incompetent. We found that excellent teachers with high performance standards placed great importance on the feedback they received from a credible evaluator—on the account rendered to them.

Even though most teachers claim that the most important indicator of their success lies in the responses of their students, external validation plays an important role. The following comments describes the power that teacher evaluation holds for recognizing excellence and validating effective performance:

> I've never had an evaluation as thorough as this before . . . it made me feel a bit more worthwhile. It really gave me a boost. You always want

acceptance, and not just from peers. It's important for the administration to give you an "atta girl" and this helps motivate you. . . . If the administration doesn't care what I do, then I'm not going to care as much either. (From a Santa Clara teacher who received an average evaluation.)

If you are a person with high standards, you need to have a pat on your back now and then. Without evaluation, I would get very few strokes on my performance and getting these strokes helps me be a better teacher and put things into perspective. This year in particular was a tough year and the positive strokes really helped me. (From a department head in Mountain View-Los Altos.)

I need the reassurance of people looking at what I am doing. If we are not looked at, we get the attitude that nobody cares. I think it can bring about a lack of motivation and I think this has happened to many teachers. (From a career candidate in Charlotte-Mecklenburg.)

I want the administration to be interested in what I am doing. . . . It gives a teacher a sense of importance when [an administrator] feels what they're doing is important enough for him to drop in to see how it is going. (From a Moraga elementary school teacher.)

I think the strength [of evaluation] is the time that the administrators take in doing evaluations. It is really used as a reward for those who do well . . . we all need positive strokes and for me, [evaluation] served as a real reward this year. . . . It was an attempt to show that he [the principal] appreciated me. He praised me tremendously and wrote careful pages and pages of detailed observations and data. (From an English teacher in Mountain View-Los Altos.)

Validation of practice—accountability in this positive sense—is equally important at the institutional level. Feedback regarding the effectiveness of district programs, especially when they achieve stated objectives, serves the same purpose for the institution that it does for teachers. So often, district administrators hear only complaints about poorly implemented policies. But when teacher evaluation becomes a central activity within a district, it generates feedback regarding the effectiveness of district programs. For example, in Moraga, administrators have a plethora of information regarding the effectiveness of the Elements of Effective Instruction (EEI) staff development program due to its integration with the teacher evaluation system. Administrators and teachers employ effective instruction terminology during the evaluation cycle, and principals clarify areas of misunderstanding. According to one administrator,

[EEI] was the best inservice ever in Moraga. The content was useful and valuable. It had something for all . . . a common way of looking at teaching—a vocabulary. We talk at faculty meetings . . . and evaluation becomes part of the clinical supervision process.

The teacher evaluation systems in the other districts generate similar feedback regarding program effectiveness. In Charlotte, teacher evaluation has validated the district's effective teaching staff-development programs of recent years and has demonstrated the value of the position of assistant principal for instruction in each school. Similar validation of the Santa Clara Unified School District's Effective Instruction and Support training program emerges as more and more principals and teachers who have both participated in the program work through an evaluation cycle together.

The experiences of the four districts we studied, in summary, demonstrate the potential of teacher evaluation for meaningful accountability—for rendering a comprehensive account of district practices—and show how accountability operates in tandem at the individual and institutional levels. However, by achieving accountability in this comprehensive sense, these districts have achieved much more. They had laid the groundwork for producing organizational and individual improvement through this same evaluation system.

IMPROVEMENT

Improvement is a complex and multifaceted concept. Yet evaluation systems with the stated goal of fostering professional improvement for teachers often assume that it is a simple process that magically follows when the teacher reads the "Recommendations for Improvement" section at the end of an observation or evaluation report. Teachers' responses to formal evaluation in our case districts are consistent with the literature on adult learning that suggests at least two stages necessary for improvement:

• recognition of potential areas of growth through a process of reflection
• motivation to change or engage in learning activities

However, improvement activities are seldom undertaken in a vacuum—teachers are members of an organization. Thus, it is important to overall institutional growth and quality that improvement efforts not only benefit the teacher but also hold the promise of contributing to the life and goals of the larger organization. Individual improvement contributes to institutional improvement only when individual and institutional goals are congruent.

The teacher evaluation efforts we examined provide abundant evidence of the capacity of a teacher evaluation system to stimulate the necessary conditions for improvement—reflection, motivation, and integration. Coupled with resources for development, the experience of these districts suggests that teacher evaluation can result in substantive change in overall organizational capacity for improvement.

Reflection

Like most professions, teaching is poorly organized to promote reflection among its practitioners (Schon, 1983). Teachers, alone in their classrooms, receive little comment on daily practice. The press of the classroom demands constant teacher attention, such that little, if any, time remains for exchange of ideas with colleagues, much less a quiet moment for thinking about practice. Further, most teachers learn at an early stage to forgo reflection which might suggest change or experimentation and concentrate instead on techniques that achieve short-term goals of classroom control or protection within the institution. Argyris notes both the irony and difficulty associated with productive reflection:

> Without reflection, there can be little learning. . . . However, reflection is not easy because most of us reflect not so much to learn as to alter our actions in order to win and not lose, in order to remain in unilateral control, and in order to protect ourselves from feeling vulnerable. (1982:456)

Reflection is a necessary first step in professional growth and improvement. Our data provide rich examples of evaluation providing not only the opportunity for reflection but also for creating an arena in which to reassess priorities. Received in a climate of trust and face-to-face communication, expert feedback provides an opportunity for teachers to stand back from the daily routine—five lessons a day, five days a week—and examine both the short- and long-term effects of their actions for their students. Teachers we interviewed stressed the importance of reflection provided through evaluation for *all* teachers, even the most skilled and experienced. Listen to the comments of teachers from each district:

Evaluation makes you sit down to think about what is really happening in your class. You say to yourself, "What am I doing?" Rarely do we have an opportunity in this profession to get introspective. But this process makes this introspection happen. It makes us think about what the purpose of our lesson is, and I think that this is very valuable. Most of this usually gets lost in the rush of day to day activities. The real value of the process is it makes you think. (From a department in Mountain View-Los Altos.)

The observer/evaluators are like holding up a mirror . . . it's like getting dressed in the morning. It's hard to know what you look like and hard to put on your makeup without a mirror. (From an elementary-school career candidate in Charlotte.)

Evaluation makes you think long and hard as you prepare for each lesson and makes you analyze what you are doing carefully. And I guess this wouldn't always be the case if you weren't participating in the [career development] program. (From a junior-high-school provisional teacher in Charlotte.)

Even strong teachers need to be challenged every now and then and the evaluation process can do this. I think the evaluation process provides a way of looking at teaching in new ways. (From a remediation team member in Santa Clara Unified.)

[Evaluation] really has made me more conscious about how I do things in my classroom. [Because of evaluation] I am much more conscious overall about my practice and I think about my lessons more systematically. . . . (From an elementary teacher in Moraga.)

The impact [evaluation] has made is that it has made me more aware of what I do and what I don't do. For example, starting a class on time. . . . I'm more aware of this and the need to do it. (From an elementary teacher in Moraga.)

To the extent that a teacher evaluation stimulates teachers to think about their practice, it can be a powerful force for self-improvement. We saw that this individual-level reflection also provided important perspective on district-level practices. School-district officials, like teachers, all too rarely reflect about long-standing policies; teacher evaluation can stimulate reflection at the institutional as well as the individual level. For example, in Charlotte, teacher evaluation as part of the Career Development Program is creating a need for staff development, according to Schlechty, "not because staff development is mandated, but because skills are mandated." Prior to career development, no mechanism existed to expose this need; no arena existed in which the district could compare organizational and professional needs. According to the director of staff development, the district has been forced to rethink the entire delivery system for their nationally acclaimed staff-development program as a result of the teacher evaluation program.

Motivation to Change

Reflection in the absence of action fosters little improvement. Action depends on individual willingness to change. Our data highlight the fact that powerful internal motivation to learn or change can be stimulated by the external pressures associated with teacher evaluation. Teachers stress the importance of an external nudge, even in the face of strong personal commitment to do the best for youngsters. In talking about the importance of evaluation as an external motivator, many teachers drew analogies from the classroom. As the veteran elementary-school teacher in Santa Clara said,

> Evaluation has an important purpose for everyone, I think it helps keep you on your toes as a teacher. [For example], I think I might sit back on my laurels. After all, I've been teaching for thirty-two years. At this stage, it would be easy for me to [relax]. Just like the kids when pressure is taken off, adults can tend to coast too. So I think the pressures of evaluation and the expectations it places on you are good.

A teacher in Mountain View-Los Altos said,

> Accountability is very important to me. I take my work very seriously. I am self-directed, but even I need a push every now and then as well—I want to grow.

Just as students need the proper "level of concern" to motivate them to learn to the best of their ability, so too does teacher evaluation as we have described it provide the impetus for teacher growth. As a teacher in Moraga remarked:

> If the level of concern [for performance] is low, people won't grow. Evaluation is a tool to place the level of concern at the right level—[and it is important to understand that] you can't grow out of fear.

Many teachers felt that teacher evaluation stimulated them and provided a necessary push to maintain their effectiveness. For example, a provisional teacher in Charlotte sees teacher evaluation in these terms:

> It is motivating. It keeps me on my toes. You aren't allowed to be sloppy. . . . [Without it], I think I would get in a rut. I'd probably get bored. Evaluation is an incentive that pushes you to improve.

One twenty-year Mountain View-Los Altos veteran who has always received acceptable evaluations stated:

> What the evaluation does is keep you from taking the easy way out and sloughing off on your job. I really think evaluation is good for education as a whole. To be honest, without evaluation, I think my job would be easier. I might not put as much work in as I do now.

By identifying specific areas for improvement and professional growth, evaluation moves teachers beyond reflection into problem-solving and concrete action.

But evaluation also stimulates action at the institutional level because each new evaluation presents a new opportunity for learning and an opportunity to define standards of acceptable practice within the district. Because of this inherent tension, evaluation can do more than motivate individuals: it can mobilize organizational action.

The tension associated with teacher evaluation and its potential for providing validation as well as amendment also enables teacher evaluation to serve an an ever-present trigger, creating a self-generating mechanism to promote organizational maintenance and problem-solving when districts take it seriously.

Unfortunately, this inherent tension in the teacher evaluation process and its potential for generating conflict disposes most school districts to pay little, if any, attention to evaluation activity. But conflict within an organization can be healthy to the extent that it stimulates discussion, reflection, and problem-solving and then motivates individuals to select a course of action that contributes to the overall health of the enterprise. Disagreements and discussions between evaluators and teachers may reveal weaknesses in district curricula, gaps in staff-development training, or a lack of clarity in effective teaching criteria. Districts committed to teacher evaluation have no choice but to act on the evidence uncovered in the evaluative setting or risk degeneration into the empty ritualism that characterizes evaluation in all too many school districts.

In Charlotte, the district has institutionalized the tension associated with teacher evaluation in the relationship between school-based advisory/ assistance teams, observer/evaluators, and the district review committees. Their joint recommendations can mobilize district resources in support of an individual or the Career Development Program itself. Their disagreements can shock the system and test the very fabric of the school district. Each year, a new test of the system will occur, and no one can predict the outcome. In one school, the evaluations of provisional teachers highlighted the degree to which extracurricular activities, especially coaching, can divert attention from classroom performance. Yet this school has traditionally relied on new staff members to fill such positions. Confronting this issue will force this school to reexamine closely its priorities and to devise new methods for administering school programs.

We encountered other examples in Charlotte where the reports of observer/evaluators conflicted with those generated by the school-based advisory/assistance teams. Rather than disrupt the system, or stimulate efforts to circumvent district policy, the disagreement stimulated reflection and problem-solving among the teachers, their peers, and their advisory/assistance team. For example, one young career candidate related the following description of a disagreement:

> One time I had an observer/evaluator [O/E] write down that the only evidence of success that my students produced was their ability to answer my questions. Now that's strange. What else did she want me to show? As it turned out, she wanted me to assign written work. As it turned out, I had just been absent for two days and the students had had two full days of nothing BUT written work. The last thing they needed was more, but the O/E didn't know this. Now I have planned to rebut that lesson and have my rebuttal placed in my file. I haven't turned it in yet because I want my API to look at it first.

But later in this same interview, this teacher proclaimed her support for the observer/evaluators:

> I think it's good that they (the O/Es) come in from the outside. The observer should not feel intimidated by the teacher that they are observing. . . . The observer/evaluators are going to be less prone to bias in their evaluations, so observer/evaluators help make the system valid and keep

bias from creeping in. . . . Holding people accountable is the beginning to bringing about improvement in the district.

In Mountain View-Los Altos, evaluation and the tension it generates has also served as a trigger, forcing both teachers and administrators to reexamine existing routines and act to change them. Increased attention to evaluation prompted wide-ranging discussions among teachers and administrators about acceptable performance levels and the proper role of evaluation. For example, standards of acceptable practice have come under scrutiny and have been raised. As one administrator put it, "We do expect a lot more of teachers than we did five years ago. . . . We believe in high standards in this district." Teachers have been forced to reexamine their own beliefs regarding teaching standards. As one teacher stated:

> I have really mixed feelings about [higher evaluative standards] because it has caused a controversy among the staff. But the way I see it, I'm an effective teacher and I want this to be a good school. I do believe that those who have been targeted through the evaluation process really deserved to be targeted.

The tension that increased attention to teacher evaluation has generated has forced this district to continually examine district practices and modify them to promote improved professional practice. Thus, recent staff-development programs, taught by Mountain View-Los Altos teachers, reflect both individual and district-wide needs as revealed in the year-end evaluation reports of teachers. Planning these staff-development programs came about as a direct result of the need to support teachers in their attempts to conform to increased professional standards within the district.

Serious attention to teacher evaluation in Moraga revealed glaring problems with the form traditionally used for year-end ratings of teachers. The formation of a committee of teachers and administrators to construct a new form came about as a direct result of evaluation reform in the district.

Transforming reflection into active problem-solving by teachers and administrators, whether in their own classrooms, in school buildings, or at the district level, becomes a natural consequence of teacher evaluation as we have described it. Evaluation rooted in expert authority taps both professionally based improvement incentives and intrinsic rewards in motivating individuals to maintain their effectiveness and strive for excellence.

And though it holds the potential for generating individual anxiety and organizational conflict, it also focuses attention on system-wide improvement needs.

Integration of Individual and Institutional Goals

Teacher evaluation can generate individual and organizational improvement because it creates an environment where reflection motivates problem-solving and concrete action. But change in individuals does not necessarily enhance organizational goals. An effective teacher evaluation system must also insure that professional improvement contributes to the life and goals of the school district. Integration of organizational and individual activities is a consequence of teacher evaluation as described here and is important to overall improvement goals. It can serve as a significant factor in the initial and continuing socialization of teachers (see Lacey, 1977:47). Teacher evaluation becomes an integration mechanism that operates across school, classroom, and individual "boundaries" to support a collaborative culture and institutional cohesion.

Teachers in each district described how the evaluation process had helped them focus their improvement efforts on the classroom. The goal-setting process that lies at the heart of each evaluation system, when approached seriously, enables teachers to integrate their own professional growth with improved classroom practice. According to one teacher, "Evaluation has helped me look back at what my own goals were [compared to those of the district] and help to keep me on track. It has refocused me."

In Moraga, virtually every teacher reported incorporating elements from the effective instruction staff-development program into their teaching repertoire. Continued focus on effective teaching techniques through the evaluation system helped to integrate new material into existing repertoires, to translate theory into practice. Teachers in the Santa Clara Unified School District reported similar experiences with the Effective Instruction and Support program in that district. According to one twenty-year veteran elementary-school teacher and remediation specialist who had just described the manner in which the principal integrated staff-development training with the formal evaluation process:

I have changed as a result of the effective teaching and clinical support program. That has changed my teaching. I can think of several areas where

I have changed my classroom instruction as a result of my participation in that program. . . . It has been important to me that the principal now comes in and can focus on specific things that I'm doing and speak in language that he and I can both understand.

In Charlotte, the new director of the Career Development Program commented that evaluation and the attendant professional development activities have ". . . opened up the classroom door."

At the institutional level, the overarching value of a teacher evaluation lies in its potential for merging organizational and professional goals. Evaluation, as a component of the formal authority structure, communicates district priorities, "what people care about." At the same time, teacher evaluation that focuses on classroom practice, professional reflection, and student learning taps powerful professional motivations and incentives. A social studies teacher in Mountain View-Los Altos, said, for example, "The goals of the district are my goals. I've always felt that, but going through the evaluations has reminded me of what I'm doing and has helped to focus me on what I should be doing in the classroom." Evaluation thus becomes the focus for individual learning within the district that contributes to the overall health of the organization.

The following statement from Charlotte-Mecklenburg's administrative staff illustrates how evaluation and the Career Development Program have become the central, unifying force there:

> The teacher career development program actually grew out of efforts to provide more effective coordination of diverse staff development components. . . . The program has merely identified these successful elements and suggested ways of organizing them to systematically improve the quality of school programs and school performance.

In this respect, evaluation is an attention-getting device. It uncovers organizational needs and focuses individual action in directions that contribute to school-system goals. It is not surprising, then, that we encountered several examples of teachers in Charlotte who had integrated their professional growth efforts with district goals and priorities. Over one-half of the career candidates in the district chose to focus their action growth plans on the new writing and math programs within the district. Several other teachers had developed new curricula, and plans were being made to share their results with other teachers in the district. In each of these cases, self-evaluations and discussions with advisory/assistance teams revealed areas where professional growth and organizational priorities came together. This district administrator, who had reviewed all of the action growth plans in her area, estimated that every teacher had focused his or her plan on at least one district-wide goal, with writing goals, math goals, and computer goals leading the way.

Advisory/assistance teams in Charlotte are another critical mechanism for integrating individuals into the organization and for providing a structure for socializing new members into the collaborative norms and values of the school system. In one school, the principal described the final summative meeting held the night before for a career candidate in the school. The meeting lasted beyond 6:00 P.M., and he likened the process to "giving birth." Together, the teacher and her advisory/assistance team had been through so much during the year and had worked so hard with the sole purpose of assisting the teacher in advancing to Career Level I status that the culmination of the process was truly an emotional experience. Eventually, Career Level I and II teachers will exclusively serve as mentors and peer members of advisory/assistance teams, thus forming a self-perpetuating system of quality control, high standards, and collaboration within the district.

The other districts we visited have less-developed mechanisms for integrating teachers with the organization through the teacher evaluation process, but we observed this effect nonetheless. For example, a science teacher in Mountain View-Los Altos had worked closely all year with the assistant principal on a district-sponsored curriculum development process. As a result, the administrator had a firm working knowledge of this particular curriculum. His assignment as the teacher's prime evaluator for the year made the evaluation process particularly useful for both individuals, resulting in a great deal of fine-tuning, adjustment, and reflection. This experience highlights the value of integrating all district-management activities into the teacher evaluation process.

There is little doubt, in sum, that teacher evaluation as it operates in the four districts in varying degrees supports reflection, motivation to change, and integration between individual and district goals. By all reports, teacher evaluation contributed significantly to individual and institutional improvement. Further, we saw that this improvement or learning extended beyond remediation of weak practice or fixing of ineffective policies to include continuing growth for effective teachers and fine-tuning of effective policies. Teacher evaluation of the sort pursued in these districts thus supports improvement of the most comprehensive variety because it represents more than running to stay in place. When extended to all teachers and to institutional activities, it represents qualitative improvement in overall district capacities.

SUMMARY

A teacher evaluation system aimed at broadly conceived accountability and improvement goals can create a self-generating mechanism for organizational and individual learning. Such a system promotes bottom-line accountability and recognition of excellence, coupled with a process of reflection on practice and problem-solving at the individual and institutional level. Evaluation thus becomes an integrating mechanism that merges organizational and professional concerns. In this way, teachers' professional growth efforts enrich the organization and help to achieve its goals.

The districts we studied, even though they were at different stages of the process of implementing teacher evaluation reform, underscore the importance of a comprehensive conception of accountability and improvement because that conception guides planning and allocation of resources for evaluation. The districts we observed also demonstrate that when accountability is approached as rendering an account for all—the exceptional, the average, and the weak—the evaluation system is more likely to be accepted as a tool for professional reflection, and improvement follows as a consequence.

Perhaps more than any organizational practice, teacher evaluation is the arena in which a school district acts out the norms and values of the organization and reveals organizational priorities. Within that arena, traditional, ritualistic teacher evaluation practices reinforce norms of isolation and conservatism. In contrast, the created culture of teacher evaluation supports coordination and integration of institutional and individual activities. And contrary to the fears of educators familiar with conventional teacher evaluation practices, teacher evaluation of this stripe supports rather than constrains professionalism.

CHAPTER 5

Teacher Evaluation
and Reflective Practice

We have examined four districts' efforts to introduce, support, and sustain a program of strong teacher evaluation. Although none has solved all of the problems associated with developing and installing a meaningful teacher evaluation effort, each district has made substantial progress toward doing so. In particular, each district has been successful in taking the first necessary step—generating teacher commitment and support for evaluation.

The teacher evaluation activities in these districts and the processes which underlie them provide valuable guidance to policymakers and practitioners. They suggest that the major source of tension and disagreement between legislators (who want accountability and quality control) and educators (who want autonomy and an increased sense of professionalism) is rooted not in a necessary reality of teacher evaluation but instead in dominant conceptions of the process and its function. The experiences we studied suggest that it is possible to think about teacher evaluation in a way that satisfies both the conditions of public trust and the needs of education professionals. To that end, three general lessons are central.

DEFINING THE RIGHT PROBLEM:
TEACHER EVALUATION AND ORGANIZATIONAL CHANGE

Teacher evaluation is primarily an *organizational* problem, not a *technical* problem. Yet, ineffective teacher evaluation efforts typically are diagnosed in terms of ineffective instrumentation, and the search for a better instrument has generated a growth industry. However, the generally successful teacher evaluation practices we studied differed on all central design dimensions and employed diverse instruments (see also Wise et al., 1984). Clearly there are no recipes for a successful teacher evaluation effort. Critical obstacles to getting started with teacher evaluation and sustaining it lie in attitudes of teachers and administrators about each other, about the role of feedback, and about the purposes of evaluation.

Organizational change of any stripe is difficult to initiate and manage. Teacher evaluation presents an organizational change problem of the most difficult sort because it requires change in basic organizational norms and values—creating and sustaining a culture for evaluation.

The experiences we observed suggest that this is a two-step process involving somewhat different issues and processes. First, it is essential to establishing the *enabling conditions* for teacher evaluation—trust and open communication. Second, it is necessary to develop strategies and processes that nurture and strengthen this commitment to meaningful teacher evaluation.

We saw that multiple factors play a role in the first step—developing enabling conditions. A triggering event functioned in each district to disrupt routines, suspend expectations about established practice, unfreeze the values and attitudes that characterized the institution. Two factors then transformed the resulting openness to organizational change into an active focus on teacher evaluation. The first factor is that comprehensive, high-priority, district-wide improvement efforts legitimized teacher evaluation. In the context of substantial district investment of resources and energy on educational improvement, concern about a strong teacher evaluation made sense to district staff. In other words, teacher evaluation achieved legitimacy in the service of improvement. This sequence of events stands in contrast to that evident in many districts in which teacher evaluation is promoted as *the* improvement effort. Claims for evaluation as "good for you" or as a means of improvement understandably fall on skeptical ears when evaluation is the apparent beginning and end of a district's investment in better practice. The second factor is that the superintendents' commitment to teacher evaluation within this context of change and improvement was essential to secure priority for evaluation and for moving ahead with planning and implementation.

But the insistence of superintendents would amount to little without other activities designed to further trust between administrators and teachers. The superintendents' management style set the necessary tone in the districts we visited; an open, accessible manner of relating with individuals at all levels of the district helped teachers to feel that evaluation was not being "done to them" particularly but that an integrated part of district-wide efforts to provide quality education was the goal. Active stakeholder participation in planning and development (and subsequently in reviewing practices) reinforced teachers' perceptions that their views and needs were taken seriously and that evaluation was indeed intended to serve rather than to police the profession. A system of checks and balances reinforced the fairness and professionalism of the evaluation system. Shared training for administrators and teachers further strengthened trust and candid communication and contributed a shared language and a common framework with which to pursue evaluation.

All of these strategies enhanced communication which, in turn, nurtured shared values and goals about evaluation and about the institution as a whole. Mobilization of commitment to evaluation and acceptance of substantive evaluation efforts requires such common values, assumptions, and goals. Consensus of this sort is essential to candor, to risk-taking, and to a willingness to act on evaluation outcomes. In particular, common values and trust make it acceptable to pass on bad news or suggestions for change. Common values underlie basic agreement about the legitimacy and value of the process as well as its fundamental benevolence (Wildavsky, 1979:236 ff).

The districts we studied also remind us that the "teacher evaluation problem" is never "solved." Creation of a culture for evaluation is the first step in establishing a strong teacher evaluation program. The second and ongoing issue is sustaining and strengthening that culture. This task requires consistent, express attention from district leadership. For example, we saw in Santa Clara how diversion of the superintendent's attention from teacher evaluation by pressures of school closings and other crises associated with enrollment decline was associated with concomitant shifts in attention on the part of administrators responsible for evaluation.

A strong teacher evaluation program also requires ongoing review and revision by stakeholders. For example, as a result of teacher suggestions, Charlotte-Mecklenburg's teacher evaluation plan has been refined since our visits. Teachers requested greater focus on classroom content and a lessened emphasis on teaching "how to"; teachers' preferences for unannounced classroom visits has prompted a greater number of evaluator drop-ins; at the same time, the number of formal conferences between evaluators and teachers has been reduced (Southern Regional Education Board, December 1986:4). As a consequence of this process of review and revising, the evaluation activity itself is strengthened as is teachers' commitment to it.

In summary, initiating, implementing, and sustaining teacher evaluation, requires, first of all, defining the right problem. Teacher evaluation is an organizationally based, not a technically based, issue. Getting started with a consequential teacher evaluation effort is a problem of organizational change. It requires new ways of thinking, new ways of doing things, new attitudes about evaluation. Sustaining a consequential teacher evaluation effort is a problem of organizational maintenance—nurturing and reinforcing the beliefs and practices essential to making it work.

Accomplishing these tasks requires a strategic combination of *pressure and support* for evaluation (see Fullan, 1986). The primary difficulty in crafting, implementing, and sustaining a strong teacher evaluation system stems from the often-dysfunctional authority relationships found in many school districts and in the resulting guarded communication between administrators and teachers. It also is a result of the general "allergy" to evaluation found in any organization. Pressure, in the form of superintendents' attention and insistence, and an accountability structure for evaluation, is essential to focus attention on evaluation. Support in the form of joint training, an open management style, stakeholder participation, and some system of checks and balances nurtures trust, shared values, and common goals for evaluation. Finding the right balance may be difficult and will necessarily reflect district traditions, expectations, and capacity. But, as Fullan warns, ". . . If you get pressure without support you get alienation; if you get support without pressure you get waste of resources" (1986:5).

ACCOUNTABILITY AND IMPROVEMENT: THE REFLECTIVE TEACHER

Conventional wisdom holds that a single evaluation system cannot serve accountability and improvement objectives simultaneously. Our observations suggest that this is not necessarily true and that traditional conceptions of accountability and improvement misspecify these terms. Further, we conclude that an evaluation system built on an assumption of incompatibility will be unable to serve either purpose as effectively as it might. We have seen that accountability and improvement are harmonious and reinforcing goals, not competing objectives. Accountability

of a fundamental kind—organizational control of the most essential stripe—
occurs *through* strategies based in improvement or learning because it is
rooted in professional norms and values.

The rationale for this apparent contradiction is highlighted by most
school districts' experience with evaluation strategies. Most teacher evaluation schemes create an organizational climate where little learning or
accountability can take place. This is true because teacher evaluation in
most districts operates as a no-win game. Teachers have incomplete information or information too general to be useful about areas in which change
is needed. They have few, if any, resources to make the changes suggested
by an evaluation. Principals lack resources to respond to their findings.
Both are afraid they will look bad; both feel they have more to lose than
gain from a strong teacher evaluation effort. Accountability, thus, is
minimal or pro forma and learning or improvement is rare.

"Winnings" under this model are slim at the institutional level as
well. Most teacher evaluation schemes assess teachers' performance against
minimum standards. This makes evaluation an irrelevant exercise for the
90–95% of the "satisfactory" teachers in the district, and so evaluation
does little to boost the quality of performance in the district's classrooms.

In this way traditional systems of evaluation distance teachers and
administrators from responsibility for problem-solving and from reflection
about practice. In such a climate neither control nor learning—neither
accountability nor improvement—can occur with any regularity or pre-
dictability. Accountability and improvement not only are compatible
objectives; they are necessary partners.

Teacher evaluation, as we have seen it operate, can serve both
improvement and accountability objectives because it joins knowledge
and power at all levels of the system from the classroom to the central
office. Thus control, in this case, is located within the individual as well
as in the institution. Further, it is control based in professional values
and motivation.

For teachers, the most powerful incentives are those related to the
achievement and development of their students (see, for example, Lortie,
1975). When benefits to their students are clear, teachers typically will
expend considerable effort in changing present practices or acquiring new
skills (see, for example, McLaughlin, 1985). Teacher evaluation systems
as we have described them establish both intrinsic and extrinsic incentives
for teachers to engage in meaningful evaluation and to act on its results.
At the broadest level, they do this because they shift the authority structure

within a school district from one based in rules and reliant on coercion and compliance—a command-and-control model—to one based in professional norms, values, and incentives. Ironically, a bureaucratic inspection system coupled with the application of external sanctions designed to improve the profession by getting rid of the "bad apples" may actually diminish the profession by frustrating competent teachers to the point of departure. Teachers' negative reactions to past evaluation practices in Moraga linked to the district's merit-pay provision in the eighteenth and twenty-third year of service illustrate this point. Because such an approach is inconsistent with teachers' incentives, it produces alienation.

In contrast, teacher evaluation of the type we have seen establishes a more effective strategy of organizational control because it aligns organizational goals with professional authority. Accountability, thus, lies in the professional orientation of teachers, a form of control much more secure when classroom doors are closed than that vested in formal roles, sanctions, or authority.

In this respect, a strong teacher evaluation system contributes to teachers' socialization in the most fundamental way. A teacher evaluation system based in common values, shared goals, open communication, and frequent interaction about classroom activities supports the type of performance most likely to reflect organizational goals and standards of best practice when teachers face students alone in the classroom. To this point, some kinds of teacher autonomy can be inimical to the goals of the organization when individual preferences and objectives are inconsistent with those of the institution. Teacher evaluation strategies, through open communication, interaction, and discussion, provide the kinds of professional stimulation and feedback that support individual growth consistent with institutional goals and values. Organizational control achieved through such normative means is the more enduring, robust, and predictable (see, for example, Wildavsky, 1979:221).

The sort of reflection associated with a meaningful teacher evaluation system also motivates teachers to challenge their own routines, to experiment with new practices, and to attend to their professional growth. Teacher evaluation can make the difference between "stuck" teachers—individuals with no sense of progress, growth, or development—and "moving" teachers—individuals who look forward, take risks, pursue growth (see Kanter, 1984, for elaboration of stuck versus moving employees in an organization). Stuck teachers tend to lower their aspirations and isolate themselves from the organization. Moving teachers aim for more and generally are highly committed to the schools and districts in which they teach. The consequence is precisely the kind of energy and concern for quality that both policymakers and practitioners want in the schools.

In summary, accountability and improvement not only are compatible objectives; they are necessary partners. Just as a combination of pressure and support is necessary to focus attention on teacher evaluation throughout the district and foster the conditions that enable, so too do teachers need both pressure and support to grow professionally. Accountability objectives provide, in teachers' words, a necessary "nudge" and institutional insistence that evaluation be taken seriously. Improvement objectives provide the support for professional goals and give authority to accountability goals. Both accountability and improvement can become empty objectives without their combined legitimacy, authority, and resources. A strategic combination of pressure and support are as important at the individual level, we see, as they are at the institutional level. They support reflective practice.

ACCOUNTABILITY AND IMPROVEMENT: THE REFLECTIVE ORGANIZATION

Teacher evaluation rooted in broadened, complementary notions of accountability and improvement not only supports reflective practice at the individual level—it supports reflection at the institutional level as well. Organizational reflection results when the outcome of an individual's evaluation is interpreted in terms of the individual *and* in terms of the context in which the individual functions.

Few school systems evaluate district-wide programs systematically. Few teachers are challenged to reflect on and improve their instructional techniques. Instead, most school districts are defensive, self-sealing systems, where trust and inquiry are low, frustration and wariness high. The organizational costs of teacher evaluation in such a setting are considerable— most particularly, hostility and frustration on the part of teachers, and support for organizational entrophy instead of growth.

But the practices we have observed suggest how teacher evaluation can become an arena for professional and organizational reflection, with teaching effectiveness at the heart of the inquiry. Teacher evaluation can be the stimulus for new learning and new problem-solving at both individual and institutional levels as individuals recognize problems, see solutions, act on them, and evaluate the results.

When the evaluation system is fully integrated into a district's management activities and policy system, teachers' attitudes and the quality of their instructional practices become the ultimate gauge of district and building-level choices. Similarly, within this institutional context, diagnosis of an individual problem is seen for what it is—diagnosis of a *systemic* problem. Thus, a problem with an individual teacher's classroom performance can be reframed as a problem with broader district practices—recruitment policies, staff-development opportunities, or supervisory practices, for example. Such a view was apparent in Charlotte, where the assistant superintendent for personnel balked at answering a question that required him to assess the effectiveness of teachers and administrators in the district. "That's really not the appropriate question," he quipped, "Our people are only as good as our district's commitment to training. Let's talk about that."

In a climate of trust and support, face-to-face communication, and commitment to the evaluation process, teacher evaluation generates information that identifies areas of institutional strength and weakness, directions for new activities, training efforts, and revisions of existing policy. Every evaluation thus comprises a test of the system. Effective teacher evaluation puts both the individual and the school district under scrutiny. It institutionalizes the inherent tension between the individual and the organization, confronting the status quo head on.

From this perspective, the reasons why technically based teacher evaluation reform efforts fail to realize both accountability and improvement goals become clear. Evaluation systems rooted in rules and procedures attempt to remove the tension inherent in the evaluation of an ambiguous enterprise like education. Technical solutions attempt to substitute decision rules for professional reflection and judgment. They establish "cut-off" scores that determine eligibility for organizationally based sanctions and use the process-product research findings regarding effective teaching for legitimation. The numbers determine evaluation outcomes. Any dissatisfaction gets channelled into debates regarding the rationality of the evaluation process, sidestepping the truly important issues that focus on definitions of effective teaching to promote student learning. Technically based evaluation reforms mistakenly attempt to remove conflict from the evaluation process.

But conflict can also be healthy in an organization, given an enabling organizational climate. A system of checks and balances that requires professionals to wrestle with evaluative judgments that must withstand the scrutiny of still other professionals institutionalizes the tension associated with evaluation and provides a forum where conflict can be aired. Thus, in Mountain View-Los Altos, commitment to high evaluative standards has indeed produced the seeds of conflict, but rather than cripple the system, the reflection and problem-solving that has resulted has made the district stronger.

Teacher evaluation conducted in an institutional context of mutual trust and support for evaluation thus initiates a cycle of reflection and self-evaluation at both the individual and institutional level. It not only provides feedback regarding individual and organizational effectiveness, but it also serves as an institutionalized trigger to stimulate routine reflection about the assumptions, norms, and values that support professional practice in a school district. Evaluation becomes self-generating because individuals are constantly sharpening their competence and ability to learn, and thus, their ability to recognize and solve problems. Evaluation in this context is *future-oriented*, not *past-focused*; it is *investment-centered*, not *pay-off* centered (see Kanter, 1984). That is, it rewards efforts to change and grow rather than to reward past "satisfactory" performance. As such it focuses on the institution as the context and resource for that development rather than on individuals' previous behavior.

At both the institutional and the individual level, the self-evaluating institution engages in learning of the most basic kind. This learning is reflected on three dimensions: *change in strategies*, as the institution modifies policies such as staff development or recruitment and the individual alters professional practices; *change in competence*, as institutional and individual areas of weak performance are addressed; and *change in aspirations*, as goals are clarified and performance is mapped against them (see, for example, Levinthal and March, 1982). It is through learning of this sort that teacher evaluation stimulates a self-renewing process of problem-solving, action and reflection that leads to accountability and improvement of the most fundamental kind.

CHAPTER 6

The Four School District Case Studies

The four school districts in this study were chosen for their commitment to installing meaningful teacher evaluation programs based on accountability and improvement objectives. While none is exemplary, each has made significant progress toward installing a strong teacher evaluation program.

STUDY METHODS

We spent approximately two to three weeks in each district except Charlotte, where our interview and observation schedule was crammed into six days. In each district, we began by contacting the district administrator responsible for teacher evaluation to obtain an overview of evaluation practices and policies. We explored district expectations, operating assumptions, implementation issues, strengths and weaknesses. We reviewed district evaluation plans, instruments and policy statements, collective bargaining agreements, training manuals and materials, and samples of completed evaluation reports. We then interviewed other district staff involved in the evaluation process, including personnel directors, superintendents, principals, teachers' organization officers, teachers, and local education news reporters.

Our sample of teachers, administrators, and schools was selected with input from central-office personnel, who offered many helpful suggestions but did not constrain the development of our final sample. The strategies we used to identify respondents varied according to district size. In the relatively small districts of Mountain View-Los Altos and Moraga, we were able to interview principals and their assistants in every school, as well as five or six teachers selected to represent a range of experience with the evaluation system. In Santa Clara, we interviewed six administrators, fourteen teachers, and three remediation team members in three of the district's twenty schools. In Charlotte-Mecklenburg, we visited four high schools, four junior high schools, and five elementary schools at different stages in implementing the Career Development Program; we spoke with eight building administrators, ten central-office personnel, and twenty-four teachers.

While we pursued issues specific to each district, we followed a common protocol in all sites. We sought perceptions of the role of teacher evaluation in improving the quality of instruction and maintaining the quality of the teacher corps. We also collected information about each community's political context, district management style, and the extent to which evaluation was coordinated with other district activities, particularly staff development.

We sought information about the role teacher evaluation played in the day-to-day life of principals and vice principals and its impact on the school's instructional program and on the professional development of teachers. We asked administrators about the issues associated with an evaluator's role in light of the district's particular evaluation policies, the implementation of formal evaluation policy, the resources available for implementation of and response to evaluation, and the ways in which teacher evaluation contributed to or obstructed their ability to attain instructional and other school goals.

From teachers, we sought an understanding of the role of evaluation in their professional lives, particularly its impact on their sense of satisfaction and efficacy, and the extent to which they felt the district's evaluation policy supported their professional goals. We were particularly interested in teachers' views on the validity, reliability, and usefulness of evaluation practices. Teachers' organization officials provided us with histories of district labor-management relations, the organization's role in developing the evaluation program, and their perception of the general response of teachers to the evaluation efforts.

The case studies that follow were submitted to district administrators for their review and comments before publication.

THE SANTA CLARA UNIFIED SCHOOL DISTRICT TEACHER EVALUATION SYSTEM

Santa Clara Unified School District is in a unique position. We have faced challenges of change as opportunities. As a result the district has been recognized for many programs and organizational processes. With a marked period of declining enrollment, the district has closed schools, reduced costs, increased cash flow, improved sites, decreased and reorganized staffs, revised and developed curriculum, established systems of district-wide goals, accountability, planning, and evaluation, and made use of multiple program resources [federal, state and private]. (SCUSD proposal for Academy for Excellence.)

The Santa Clara Unified School District (SCUSD), which lies south of San Francisco in the heart of the Silicon Valley, was established in 1966 as a consolidation of four smaller districts. It is comprised of fifteen schools and an adult education center, which operate with an annual budget of approximately $44 million. Thirteen thousand students are dispersed in two senior high schools, two junior high schools, ten elementary schools, and a continuation high school.

Over the last decade, declining enrollments and a fiscal crunch caused by the 1978 passage of Proposition 13 have challenged district management. Fifteen schools have been closed since 1974, and two major school reorganizations have occurred. Some sites have been closed and others leased, producing revenue which has been used to renovate existing facilities and maintain instructional programs. Due in part to reductions in the teaching force, teachers at the bottom of the seniority list show fifteen years of experience and an average age of fifty-three. Teaching salaries have increased an average of 5% every year over the past decade, putting Santa Clara in the top six of the surrounding school districts in Santa Clara County. Salaries range from $20,000 for a beginning teacher to $37,000 for a thirty-year veteran.

The surrounding community contains a mixture of high, middle, and low socioeconomic status areas and a diversity of ethnic groups. Nineteen percent of the student population is of Hispanic origin, and 13% is of Asian descent. The increase of these minority enrollments in the past decade, from 20% to over 40% overall, has forced the district to confront racial integration issues and to modify its curricular offerings. A concerted effort by teachers and administrators and major curricular reforms were effective in turning around a downward trend in achievement test scores during the first five years of this period, and 1983–1984 saw a rise in student performance in the California Assessment Program from the 52nd to the 67th percentile.

Despite these external changes, district management and the local teachers' organization, an NEA affiliate, share a positive relationship, cooperating extensively during the recent district reorganization and providing a stability which effectively counteracted the turbulence from without. According to a union official, "The teachers' association has worked very closely with the district to solve problems. The relationship has been very positive."

Community Relations,
Shared Governance, and Accountability

Establishing trust between parents, teachers, and administrators within the district has not been easy. The referendum that brought about the consolidation of four smaller school districts to form the Santa Clara Unified School District passed by only thirty-five votes. In its first eight years, the district saw three superintendents come and go before the present superintendent, Rudi Gatti, assumed control in 1974. Gatti attributes his long tenure in part to his efforts to address communication and community relations problems and resource constraints, as well as his belief in the fundamental importance of teacher evaluation.

Gatti believes that teachers had unfairly taken the brunt of the criticism and blame during the district's early years. Because he had once served as personnel director within Santa Clara, he knew the territory well:

> Before I decided to take the job, I sat down with the Board and we talked about what we thought were priorities in the district and what needed to be done. Before I took the job, I got a commitment from the Board to what my agenda was going to be for bringing about a situation that would have teachers treated fairly. . . . I wouldn't have taken the job if I had not gotten that commitment from them.

Gatti's first and most important agenda item was to open channels of communication between the board of education, his management team, and the teachers. He turned to an old colleague, Donald Thomas, Superintendent of the Salt Lake City Public School System, and secured his services as a management consultant for the district for the next seven years. Gatti hoped to adapt Thomas's philosophy of shared governance to Santa Clara. Gatti continues to refer to the relationship between the teachers' union and the board of education as a "shared governance" contract.

Thomas met separately with members of the board and the management team to discern the areas of agreement and dissent. He was able to establish a consensus of goals and priorities by emphasizing common-alities. An important outcome of this process was a commitment to establish a remediation program for poorly performing teachers, modeled after the Salt Lake system.

Gatti made strategic use of declining enrollments and the necessity to close some schools. Advance planning and astute real estate management were important factors to his success. As one teacher put it,

> We have done a lot of things in this district ahead of other districts. We've looked to the future. We closed schools here long before districts around here ever did because we saw the coming problems that would result if we didn't. There were lots of committees around the district looking for a closing, where we should close schools, how many, and as a result we saved a lot of money. Rudi Gatti is a very good businessman and that's the way it should be. Educators don't always know a lot about renting and leasing schools and how to be real estate managers. Rudi is really good at this.

Gatti was able to turn these properties into sources of revenue for the district—slack resources he could call on to support change efforts such as teacher evaluation. (The overall fiscal health of Santa Clara can be contrasted to neighboring San Jose, which declared bankruptcy several years ago.) When these school closures caused a strain in district/community relations, Gatti's solution was to establish an accountability system to keep the board and community informed about how well the district was meeting its goals.

The Santa Clara Unified School District's evaluation system is based on the belief that accountability should flow all the way through a school system. According to one district administrator, "It's sort of a chain reaction, flowing from the Superintendent, through us, to the principals and teachers." An annual needs assessment survey is administered to a sample of students, parents, and staff members. Evaluation of district programs at both building and district level is based upon these data, along with the results of student achievement testing. The superintendent reports the results in an "Annual Progress Report to the Community." Teachers and administrators then establish goals for the following year based on priorities set by the board.

Parent satisfaction with district performance in the areas of basic academic skills, school discipline, attendance procedures, pupil respon-sibility, and instructional and administrative leadership has steadily climbed over the years to a high of over 90% in the spring of 1984. Administrators believe that the accountability program is crucial in maintaining community support because it provides a vehicle for communication and participation at all levels of the system.

Superintendent Gatti had held a vision of the potential role of teacher evaluation in any school improvement program since his tenure as a high-school principal. He believed that teacher evaluation could be a means to establishing teachers' trust. He described the roots of his vision this way:

> I can remember when I was a principal, I really didn't have any special skills regarding evaluating teachers and I probably didn't put as much energy into it as I could. But then one day I decided that it was worth making a commitment to teacher evaluation because it would get me into the classrooms and help me to improve the instructional program in my school. I started spending a lot more time and energy on evaluation, but it was only because I decided personally to make a commitment to it.

The evaluation system is equally well endorsed by teachers. Superintendent for instruction Louis Martini summed things up this way:

> [Evaluation] works because [the management team] has a good working relationship with the teachers. I think now we're almost on an extended honeymoon. I don't think relations could get much better. It's not uncommon for one of us to get a note from a teacher thanking us for the kinds of things we do in the district. They really appreciate us . . . I think there is a lot of trust in this district.

Gatti and the board of education have received national recognition for these accomplishments. The *Executive Educator Magazine* recently selected Gatti as one of the top 100 school administrators in America, and the U.S. Department of Education designated the Santa Clara School Board as one of twenty exemplary boards in the nation.

Evaluation Strategies

This statement from the SCUSD Uniform Evaluation System manual describes the district's philosophy on teacher evaluation:

> Evaluation is a positive process which aids professional educators to improve skills related to their areas of responsibility. The entire process involves

describing professional responsibilities, assessing performance, comparing this performance with established standards, and providing assistance for improving performance. An additional intent of evaluation, as set forth in the Stull-Rodda Professional Competency Act, is to promote and document the accountability of district certificated employees. The employee and the entire system will be held accountable for its high mission of educating its children and youth.

This statement reflects a philosophy of evaluation common to school districts across the country, of the joint purposes of professional improvement and accountability for acceptable performance levels. Santa Clara implements this philosophy in the following manner:

The policy and procedures of teacher evaluation are outlined in a district manual, "Certificated Employees Uniform Evaluation System." Teachers begin the process each year by submitting a list of objectives. Administrators observe classroom teaching at least twice. Conferences occur subsequent to each observation and at the end of the year, when the teacher receives a summative rating of "effective," "needs improvement," or "remediation required" in each of seven categories:

1. The teacher as assessor of student needs;
2. The teacher as planner of instruction;
3. The teacher as presenter of instruction;
4. The teacher as controller;
5. The teacher as evaluator of student progress and instructional purposes;
6. The teacher as communicator of the educational process;
7. The teacher as professional.

Under each category, four to eight statements further explicate role expectations. If a teacher is found to be needing improvement or formal remediation, the administrator must provide additional documentation. Evaluators may also attach commendations for any area of the teacher's performance. Tenured teachers undergo evaluation every other year, beginning the cycle by reviewing their previous evaluation results.

This process differs little from that found in many school districts across the nation. This system is noteworthy in two areas: its incorporation of staff development in teacher evaluation, and its formal remediation process.

STAFF DEVELOPMENT

During the past three years, Santa Clara has dramatically increased the number of staff-development opportunities available for teachers and administrators. The complete funding of staff development is now included in the district's operating budget, and a full-time staff-development specialist coordinates the program.

The focus on staff development began with the support of a Packard Foundation grant, when Santa Clara initiated a program for both teachers and administrators based on the instructional variables of the effective schools research. Entitled "Effective Instruction and Support" (EIS), this program facilitates the mastery of new skills and concepts by participants through a system of observation, feedback, and coaching. EIS represents a major shift in the focus of staff development and evaluation strategies. Based on the responses of teachers and administrators within the district, the impetus for this recent focus on staff development relates to the composition of the professional workforce and their developmental needs. According to one remediation team member in the district:

> Six or seven years ago, some teachers had some horrible problems and so we set out to fix them with remediation. Now, with clinical teaching, we are not just focusing on the bottom end. Now the focus is to make all teachers more effective so that people don't even get to the stage where they need remediation at all. . . . I think it is very important for any teacher to be refreshed at certain times during their career.

Coupled with an emphasis on maintaining the effective performance of experienced teachers is a concern for an anticipated influx of new teachers that will accompany the anticipated increase in student population and the retirement of a large cadre of older teachers. According to one district administrator:

> The emphasis these days in this district is on staff development, not remediation so much, and one of the reasons for this is that we're going to need to concentrate on new teachers in the near future. . . . We want to train these new teachers and pick up where the universities have not always done a super job. We want to use our better teachers and we want to develop their skills as teachers through clinical supervision.

A committee of district administrators and teachers conducts the program and serves as coaches. After a three-day classroom session, participants team up with a trained coach who assists them in developing and presenting a lesson based on effective teaching principles grounded in the work of Madeline Hunter. The coach provides critical feedback and support through classroom observations and conferences for three lessons. Teachers also have a variety of resources at their disposal, including a collection of written and videotaped lessons prepared by prior participants, which serve as models and instructional aids.

Teachers who have received the training are unanimous in their praise. The direct instructional model serves to validate effective practices already employed in the classroom. Several teachers have indicated that the experience brought about improvement in their performance. According to one sixteen-year veteran junior high-school teacher,

> I really believe that I did change the way I teach as a result of my participation [in the EIS program]. It forces you to break down the teaching task into tiny steps, and by doing this, I realized where I was jumping too far ahead of the kids. I really believe the kids learn more as a result.

All district administrators, including the superintendent, have received the training and have taught several lessons in district classrooms. As a result, and in compliance with California law, all administrators have become certified evaluators. Approximately a quarter of the district's teachers have participated to date, and Gatti promises that all certified personnel will eventually complete the program.

EIS is coupled with the evaluation process in the district in several ways. In some cases, administrators have actively employed the EIS techniques in their evaluations of teachers, and many teachers have asked their principals to be their coaches. One veteran high-school administrator states,

> All those things they teach you in EIS help me in my observations. . . . they give me something to focus on. So I've been able to tie EIS into my regular observations because now I can focus on the introduction to the lesson, the words the teacher uses, and how they follow through. Now I can dissect what the parts of a lesson are.

Two-thirds of the building administrators interviewed felt that the EIS training has dramatically improved their skills as evaluators. According to one assistant principal,

> Looking back to the past, I have to say that I did a poor job [of evaluating teachers] because I had no skills in the area. But then I got involved in

the EIS program. For the first time, I felt like I saw a good teaching model . . . it has given me some excellent tools that I can use in evaluation. Before, I can say that I would focus on things . . . that I really cannot say were related to teaching. . . . Now I really focus on pedagogical processes.

An evaluator's use of EIS techniques is helpful particularly when the teacher has also undergone EIS training. As one teacher put it:

I think that this has helped us both look at teaching in a similar way. . . . Knowing that we both participated made a difference because most administrators have been out of the classroom so long it means a lot to know that your evaluator has had to participate in some kind of actual teaching experience. I think it helped give him a different perspective this year. It sort of served as a refresher course for him.

The connections between staff development and evaluation in Santa Clara are loose. Some administrators report that they have transferred few EIS techniques to their formal evaluations of teachers. While some evaluators link the two, the guidelines for the uniform evaluation process make no mention of EIS. One administrator indicated that many principals were resistant to the adoption of new evaluation skills. It seems clear that the district could benefit from the provision of some additional follow-up activities. One individual who had been recruited as an EIS trainer admitted that only after additional training did she begin to incorporate its precepts into her evaluation activity.

THE REMEDIATION PROCESS

Teachers and administrators who attended the 1975 management retreat conducted by Donald Thomas emerged committed to installing a peer assistance-based evaluation system for the professional staff. A committee of teachers and administrators spent two years designing and implementing a remediation program for SCUSD based upon Thomas's Salt Lake City model. Teacher involvement in the planning process was extensive; in fact, the committee which drafted the remediation guidelines was chaired by a teacher. Teachers perceived their involvement as an opportunity to refocus the district's recently constructed evaluation system toward a philosophy of assistance and support. According to one committee member:

There was a need felt among teachers to improve evaluation in the district. Back at that time, there were many principals around who did very little if any evaluation and it became clear to us that if you were going to do a first class job with evaluation, administrators are going to have to know their business. . . . It was sort of a professional thing among teachers. There wasn't really a huge community or board of education outcry to weed out incompetence; we just felt that we wanted to police our own ranks.

When they saw the Salt Lake City program in action, it became evident to committee members that, handled unwisely, remediation could be a negative rather than a beneficial process and that the Salt Lake City program would require modifications to work for Santa Clara. According to another committee member:

We saw a lot of problems in Salt Lake City. They were putting people on remediation because they had been put into an impossible situation. . . . That's grossly unfair, and we were particularly tuned in to those kinds of problems here because our enrollment started to decline. We knew that teachers would be forced to move around because of riffing [Reductions in Force] and seniority causing people to have to teach in areas that they weren't necessarily experienced in.

Committee members were sold on the concept of a program involving remediation teams composed of teachers. They believed that this represented the best insurance that the evaluation program would retain a positive, supportive focus. The Santa Clara school board approved the committee's plan. Seventy-five teachers were nominated by their peers to serve as potential remediation specialists.

Two strategies were instrumental in the remediation program's successful implementation. The first was evidence of the superintendent's commitment. When principals did not recommend a single teacher during the program's first year, Gatti placed four principals on formal remediation for their failure to carry out their evaluation responsibilities. During the following year, ten teachers were placed on formal remediation. Holding administrators accountable was critical to making the system function.

A second important strategy was visible proof of the program's success. The first teacher to undergo formal remediation represented an important test case for the district. Though the remediation team recommended retention with some modification in teaching assignment, the feedback this individual received was instrumental in his decision to resign. Yet both teacher and administrators expressed their complete satisfaction with the final outcome—an unusual occurrence prior to the remediation program.

Any certificated employee, whether teacher or administrator, may be referred by his or her supervisor for formal remediation if informal attempts to improve deficient performance fail. Before any employee may be placed on remediation, a supervisor must document how the employee has been informed of his or her deficiencies and must be provided with assistance. A principal may provide direct supervision, refer a teacher to district-wide inservice programs, or ask for assistance from a department head or mentor teacher. At many schools, principals can use School Improvement Program (SIP) money to support staff members' remedial efforts. One principal, for example, provided tuition for a teacher for a class at a local university to improve a particular aspect of the teacher's performance. If such attempts to secure improvement fail, formal remediation results.

Two meetings initiate the formal remediation process. The first involves the teacher and the assistant superintendent for personnel. At this time the teacher is informed about the mechanics of the process and its consequences and selects members of the remediation team. A list of volunteer teachers and administrators is maintained by the personnel office for the teacher to choose from, though others may serve if the assistant superintendent and teacher agree.

If the individuals selected to serve on the remediation team agree to participate, a second meeting, involving the assistant superintendent for personnel, the remediation team, and the teacher occurs for a discussion of the upcoming remediation period. The team begins the sixty-day process by reviewing the documentation of the teacher's deficiencies with the administrators. Within reason, remediation team members have access to any resources that they deem necessary in assisting the teacher. Professional reading materials, access to professional workshops, the hiring of substitutes to allow for visitations, and other instructional aids are frequently utilized. The team's actions must be thoroughly documented. While all parties receive copies of documentation, strict confidentiality is maintained. Observations and conferences occur frequently. The extent and form of intervention depends upon the teacher's needs and upon the remediation team. At the end of the remediation period, the team presents its findings and decides whether the remediation has been successful. The remediation team's responsibility ends with this determination. The ultimate responsibility regarding the future employability of the teacher rests with the superintendent.

The remediation process is not mentioned in the collective bargaining agreement between the teachers and the school board. A teacher may not file a grievance to protest an evaluation outcome; only deviations from negotiated evaluation procedures are permissible as grievance topics. A teacher may, however, request to have a union representative present at the initial conference with the assistant superintendent for personnel. While this has not occurred to date, the union would become involved only if the administration violates any of the evaluation procedures in the collective bargaining agreement or if the teacher wishes to contest a decision for dismissal.

In the past ten years approximately twenty-six teachers have been placed on formal remediation, one-half voluntarily resigning as a result. The remaining individuals have achieved successful evaluation. The assistant superintendent for personnel, Nicholas Gervasse, points out, however, that these figures understate the impact of the remediation process on achieving district accountability goals. He offers several examples of teachers who never participated in the remediation process but who, nonetheless, resigned when faced with the possibility. The possibility of being placed on formal remediation provides a clear, unambiguous message regarding the unacceptability of a teacher's performance and serves to eliminate some incompetent teachers from the district.

Teachers acting as remediation specialists believe that, as peers, they are in a much better position than administrators to assist other teachers in improving their performances. For example, one remediation team member stated:

> In looking over the administrative evaluations done [of the teacher undergoing remediation], they were right on target about what his problems were and their recommendations for improvement. But the teacher put up such a barrier that anything they suggested didn't do any good. But he's been real receptive to us as remediators.

Remediation specialists feel well-supported by the district and have no problems gaining access to any resources they feel necessary to assist the teacher. According to one remediation specialist, "I got a blank check agreement that I could use all the substitute time I wanted and that the teacher could have a substitute if she wanted to observe us."

Remediation specialists also express the belief that an administrator should never allow teachers to deteriorate to the levels of incompetence that they have observed in the teachers with whom they work. They believe that their efforts to assist a teacher would have a much greater chance of succeeding if principals could call them in earlier in the process. As one told us:

> Principals just wait too long [before referring a teacher for remediation] and I think this is because it is very difficult to document extensively a teacher's weaknesses. A poor teacher gets to be too poor for too long before they're finally referred. . . . This teacher is so poor, she is so far off the mark, she needs total retraining.

Teachers in the district share a sense of pride and professionalism regarding the formal remediation process:

> This is the way we want things to be in the profession.
>
> Remediation is a very positive aspect of the system.
>
> I think it is good professionally to have it in place.
>
> There's a need, I believe, to police our own ranks. It's important that teachers see other teachers who need help getting that help. A strong instructional program and a strong profession needs to have people doing a good job and receiving support and assistance if they need it.

Despite the positive response the remediation program evokes, teachers and some administrators believe it is underutilized. Some respondents believe that the district could benefit from additional training in the remediation process: such training has not been available since the program's inception in 1978. While every administrator and a majority of teachers believe that incompetent teachers still exist, less than 3% of Santa Clara's teachers received a rating of "improvement needed" in at least one of the seven areas on the final evaluation form, and only one principal placed a teacher on formal remediation in 1984–1985. Some believe the cause of this problem is the disinclination of some principals to make teacher evaluation an active priority. According to assistant superintendent for personnel, Nicholas Gervasse,

Principals always seem to be the weak link in the system. . . . The [reme-diation] program is really waning now—this year we only had one teacher placed on remediation, and I feel that there should be more, maybe 5 or 6. I don't think we've given enough attention to it recently.

According to Donald Callagon, deputy superintendent in charge of plant and operations who supervises seven district principals,

Even with having the policies that we have and the availability to a rem-diation process, dismissal is still a tedious task. It's very, very difficult, almost impossible to pursue a dismissal. So I think a lot of principals just say, "The hell with it!" and go and put Satisfactory on a form and that's it.

Progress to Date

Superintendent Gatti has publicly committed himself to reading and signing every evaluation report in the coming year in an effort to focus attention on the process and hold principals strictly accountable for quality evaluations. He states:

The real problem with evaluation is that people are gutless. You can have the best teacher evaluation system in the world, but if you don't have principals and administrators who are committed to it, it just isn't going to fly.

Meeting evaluation report deadlines in accordance with the collective bargaining agreement appears to serve as the primary criterion in judging administrative competence in evaluation. Prior to the introduction of the EIS program, few principals received any systematic critical feedback from their superiors on the quality of their evaluation methods or results. As one central-office administrator with the responsibility for evaluating prin-cipals put it:

I suppose we should get copies of the evaluations [of teachers written by building administrators] here, but we don't, so we have to rely on [the Assistant Superintendent for Personnel]. This may be a weak point in our process.

Though Gatti and Gervasse emphasize the continued attention to evaluation, they indicate that the massive district reorganization in 1981, involving the transfer of over half of the professional staff, prevented them from focusing as much attention on teacher evaluation as they had in the past. According to Gatti:

> I certainly don't put as much time into [evaluation] as I used to. I've just gotten bogged down with too many other things. When something like evaluation stops being the top priority of the person at the top, it starts to fall away.

To insure that administrators attend to evaluation, all final teacher evaluation reports cross the desk of the assistant superintendent of personnel. Teacher evaluation is one of several components that comprise an administrator's year-end evaluation, but building administrators are not directly evaluated by the assistant superintendent for personnel.

The amount and quality of administrative attention placed on evaluation varies somewhat from school to school, with high schools displaying the greatest variation. As one district staff-development specialist puts it,

> It depends on the tone that the principal sets in the school. If the principal has set a positive tone, then evaluation and staff development can easily be linked together.

Several teachers have complained about the cursory nature of the evaluation they recently received. One teacher described her current evaluation this way:

> I only had one observation, but I never had a chance to sit down with my evaluator and look at what he wrote. This year, he just caught me in the hall and said, "I'm going to drop in and see you sometime this week." Then, two weeks later he dropped into my class unannounced for half the period. Several days later, he dropped by my office and asked me if I had all my [state-mandated evaluation forms completed and filed]. When I said yes, he said, "Well, that's good, you had a great observation." Now that was the extent of my evaluation.

There is some sense that evaluators only have enough time to provide comprehensive evaluations for teachers known to be having problems. As one teacher said:

This year my evaluator decided that I already do the job that he wants done and so he just didn't have the time to spend on me. Instead, he had to spend it on teachers who were in greater need.

Other teachers report that evaluation has been a powerful force in their professional development. A junior high-school teacher who had received average ratings commented:

I've never had an evaluation as thorough as this before and I think the result for me is that it made me feel more worthwhile. . . . It really gave me a boost.

For others, evaluation was a validating experience, as evidenced by the comments of this department coordinator:

I think it's important for the administration to give you an "atta boy" or an "atta girl" and this helps motivate you and reinforces the fact that you're good. I know that the principal respects me for what I do because she commented on each area of the evaluation and documented all the comments that she made.

In virtually every instance where teachers found their evaluation process to be a positive experience for professional growth, both they and their evaluators had completed the EIS training. For example, one high-school special education teacher tells us:

Both [the evaluator] and I have participated in the EIS program. I think that this has helped us both look at teaching in a similar way. . . . I think it made the whole evaluation experience more valuable for me . . . because most administrators have been out of the classroom so long, it means a lot to know that your evaluator has had to participate in some kind of actual teaching experience. . . . It gives us some basics that we can both focus in on.

The process of sharing and coaching increases teachers' feelings of efficacy and removes a measure of uncertainty from teaching. Another teacher with over twenty years of teaching experience expressed her feelings this way:

It has been important to me that the principal now comes in and can focus on specific things that I'm doing and speak in language that he and I can both understand. Most importantly, he is able to validate what I am doing and I find that very reinforcing. I think I know that what I'm doing is good, but it's important that an outside observer comes in and basically puts that rubber stamp and says "Yes, you're on the right track."

Santa Clara's experience with teacher evaluation demonstrates the critical importance of principals in implementing any program. Inadequate attention to teacher evaluation by district management sends a message to principals that spending time on evaluation is not valued; subsequent inattention to evaluation at the building level relays a similar message to teachers. If a district values teaching excellence, it allocates resources to insure that classroom effectiveness is maintained. When evaluative feedback is carefully documented and comes from a credible source, such as the EIS program, evaluation serves to validate effective practice and professional improvement. Teachers embrace accountability standards when they are contained in a program, such as formal remediation, which reinforces professional standards of effectiveness.

THE MOUNTAIN VIEW–LOS ALTOS UNION HIGH SCHOOL DISTRICT TEACHER EVALUATION SYSTEM

The Mountain View-Los Altos Union High School District serves approximately 3,000 students in grades 9 to 12 who reside in the Silicon Valley south of San Francisco. While many residents occupy high-tech professional positions, a substantial minority population at one end of the district contributes to an overall picture of ethnic and economic diversity in the schools. Even in the midst of the economic hardships endured by California schools in the wake of Proposition 13, the district takes pride in its ability to maintain a curriculum that serves the needs of this diverse student population.

Student achievement is high in Mountain View-Los Altos: approximately 75% of the students attend a two- or four-year college upon graduation, with most of the remainder securing local full-time jobs. Student test scores are well above California averages, and approximately 20% of district graduates receive a grade of 3 or better on advanced placement exams.

Parents take an active role in their children's educations. In 1984–1985, for example, the Mountain View-Los Altos Education Foundation raised over $48,000 to finance the remodeling of science facilities at both of the district's high schools. Each school employs a part-time parent coordinator to manage the talents of approximately 100 volunteers in a variety of functions. Parents demand excellence from their schools and are willing to commit time and money to ensure it.

The district employs 200 teachers with an average age of forty-three and an average experience level of fourteen years. Teachers' salaries range from $18,000 to $35,000, ranking close to the median among surrounding districts. A 40% decline in student enrollment since 1968 has reduced the number of professional staff, but the pace of retirements and resignations has meant that the district has not been forced to lay off any teachers. With enrollments increasing slightly, the district anticipates hiring new teachers in the coming year.

Despite declining enrollment and fiscal retrenchment, Mountain View-Los Altos has managed to retain some level of stability. Superintendent Paul Sakamoto recently reported that mission and goal statements produced by students, parents, community members, and staff members in 1973 continue to describe accurately current district priorities.

District administrators and representatives of the District Teachers' Association (DTA), National Education Association (NEA) affiliate, characterize their relationship as positive but "typically adversarial." While a strike has never occurred, contract settlements are rarely reached prior to the start of the school year. Until recently, increased administrative attention to teacher evaluation has been a significant issue for the teacher's union.

The case of Mountain View-Los Altos illustrates the potential difficulties a district may encounter in establishing a new evaluation system, in turning an ineffective, basically ritualistic process into a process with real standards, and how a system intended for professional development may precipitate adverse relations between teachers and administrators.

Strong Leadership

The current superintendent, Dr. Paul Sakamoto, has played a major role in evaluation reform in Mountain View-Los Altos. According to one department head:

> [Sakamoto] really runs things in this district. His philosophy pervades the whole district and he sets the style.

Staff members refer to the superintendent as "an expert manager," "an instructional leader," "a friend," "a caring human being who is tireless in his devotion to the school district." According to one teacher, it is not uncommon to find him eating lunch with students in the school's courtyard at noon. Another teacher comments:

> The Superintendent is totally committed to this district. He is single, and he makes it very clear that the district is his family as far as he's concerned. He is well respected by the staff.

Sakamoto's management style reflects a commitment to open communication and a recognition of individual work. His "Management Practices Plan," written in 1981, describes a set of administrative guidelines to develop "a unique organizational culture which believes in excellence through people and which develops a sense of family among its members." Sakamoto believes in adhering to such practices as sensitivity to individuals' feelings; an open-door policy; making the academic department the unit upon which loyalty, pride, and commitment can be built; and seeking answers to problems from those most directly involved; and he believes that these practices will produce higher morale, improved performance, greater satisfaction, and an overall increase in the achievement level of Mountain View-Los Altos students. Sakamoto's comprehensive management plan was adapted from Japanese and American management techniques that have been proven effective in industry and business. These principles, in fact, parallel management practices in local Silicon Valley high-tech firms.

Teacher evaluation was perceived as an important aspect of district management activity even prior to his superintendency, but Sakamoto sees teacher evaluation as a natural corollary to his management philosophy:

> Evaluation is the key to any comprehensive program of instructional improvement . . . the key to what goes on in schools. If high levels of student achievement are really our goal, then we should be focusing here. Teachers feel isolated, that no one cares, and just close the door. Evaluation opens the door up.

Evaluation Strategies

The purpose of teacher evaluation, as stated in Mountain View-Los Altos' collective bargaining agreement, is to improve instruction and encourage professional development. It is further understood that this purpose can be more readily achieved by a manifest willingness on the part of the parties to the evaluation process to improve instruction in a spirit of mutual trust and professionalism.

Administrators adhere to this philosophy. Teachers, however, are divided in their assessment of how evaluation is actually utilized by the district. A 1984 survey by the District Teachers' Association found that a majority of teachers believed evaluation was conducted either "to satisfy the state legal requirements or to harass teachers." Several administrators acknowledge that evaluation had taken on a "legalistic" focus in the past several years. According to one:

> I actually get two messages from the district as an administrator about evaluation. The first is that it is supposed to help teachers improve. But I also get the message that we are supposed to document things so that our evaluation process will stand up against a grievance. Our evaluations serve as a data collection base that can be used to document what is going on. For me, the dichotomy between these two purposes is incompatible.

Prior to the passage of the Stull bill in 1971, which requires that all California school districts establish uniform evaluation and assessment systems, evaluation in Mountain View-Los Altos was more ritual than substance. To rate teacher performance, principals filled out a checklist at the end of the year, typically without formal classroom observation.

After the passage of the Stull bill, the district experimented with several evaluation models, including a collegial system where teachers could select a peer to work with the principal in conducting classroom observations and offering suggestions for professional improvement. Several teachers recall that this process had a positive impact on their performance. While negotiating the first collective bargaining agreement, however, district administrators and the teachers' union agreed to abandon this practice. Evaluation was limited to administrative purview, and the formative aspects of the evaluation process were channelled into the development of a strong staff-development program.

One primary means for assessing teacher performance, still utilized today, is a student survey. The original instrument and subsequent revisions were accomplished by a cooperative effort of teachers and administrators. Students rate their teacher from weak to very strong on forty separate items in the following ten categories:

1. Teacher preparation
2. Student-teacher relationship
3. Individual needs of students
4. Teaching methods
5. Clarity of communication
6. Control of the class
7. Classroom atmosphere
8. Class procedures
9. Ideas and skills to be learned
10. Value of skills taught

This information is currently used along with several other performance indicators to arrive at a final evaluative judgment.

In accordance with California law, most teachers are evaluated only every other year. The evaluation process begins in September, when teachers are informed of the identity of their primary evaluator, who may be either the principal, assistant principal, or dean of students. Approximately sixty teachers undergo formal evaluation in each of the district's schools each year.

In September, principals publish a detailed letter informing teachers of the evaluation's procedural requirements. Each teacher prepares a list of objectives to serve as the evaluation's basis. Objectives must address at least three areas: teaching of subject content, maintaining learning environment, and other school-related activities. A teacher's objectives are unique to the challenges of the curriculum, students, and teacher's teaching style required. One "Special Day Class" teacher's list, for example, reads:

1. Each student in the Special Day Class will have an Individual Education Program (IEP) which will be addressed to the student's academic and behavioral strengths and weaknesses. The IEPs will be based on teacher assessment, standardized tests, informal tests, parental observation, and psychologist input. The student will be part of the process.
2. The classroom will be structured to facilitate learning and create optimal opportunity for success to maintain a commitment from the students to their education and show improved classroom behavior and attendance.

3. Each student will have a daily academic schedule based upon a curriculum developed to meet their academic needs and transcript deficiencies.
4. Each student will be involved in one reading assignment daily.
5. Each student will be aware of vocational opportunities. The student will also have experience in the following: filling out job applications, awareness of job training programs, and interviewing techniques where appropriate.
6. Each student will be assigned homework twice a week.

Teachers must refer to previous evaluation results and address any recommended areas for improvement. As part of the feedback loop between staff training and evaluation, the content of staff-development workshops and curriculum guides are intended to serve as guidelines in the preparation of objectives in the areas of content, learning environment, and instructional methods.

Assessment methods for all objectives must also be specified. Administrators gather documentary evidence in the following ways:

• Evaluators conduct a minimum of two classroom observations which may or may not be announced. Most teachers are observed three times; teachers experiencing difficulty may be observed as many as eight times. Post-observation conferences are standard practice.
• Teachers submit student work samples, including test results, sample projects, and homework assignments. Most administrators ask for samples from students of ranging ability.
• Student achievement data in the form of grading distributions are inspected. Comparisons are made within and across departments to reveal identifiable, persistent patterns to document student progress. An agreement with the District Teachers' Association precludes the direct use of student test scores on district-wide criterion-referenced achievement tests to evaluate teachers.
• Student survey results provide a wide range of data which are used to assess teacher performance. Teachers may administer the survey themselves or ask their evaluator to administer it. Each school receives a school-wide teacher-by-teacher summary of the student's ratings of teachers.

• Additional methods may include teacher self-assessments, teacher products such as tests and worksheets, student interviews, and anything else agreed to by teacher and evaluator.

Specifications within the collective bargaining agreement require that evaluations of probationary teachers be completed by the end of February and tenured teachers by the beginning of May. Most data are collected in the first semester of the school year. As the deadline approaches, administrators check to ensure that teachers have submitted all of the documentary evidence agreed upon in their objective-setting conferences. Evaluators then examine the data to determine the extent to which teachers have accomplished their objectives.

Evaluators must use their own judgment in weighting the various documents of teachers' performances. There is no standard formula. Administrators agree that approaching the data in a qualitative manner strengthens the overall process. They point out that judgment is needed to take the specific context—subject area, teacher experience, class composition—into account so that a rating can be computed. Administrators appear to approach the data in a similar manner. The following description is fairly typical:

> The first thing I do is lay [all the information] out on the table—the last year's evaluation, grade summary, the objectives we negotiated, the examples of student work, the results of the student survey, my observations that I conducted—and I reread all of it and write up the final summative evaluation according to a format that I have developed myself. I start out talking about the teacher's preparation and then go through all the objectives and document them whether or not they have met them. . . . I then summarize the entire student survey and make any additional commendations and recommendations at the end of this based on everything that I've said beforehand.

Another administrator prepares a draft report and then allows the teacher to review it and provide input before she writes the final evaluation. If any of the evidence appears to conflict, it is noted in this report.

Final reports are prepared along district guidelines. They range from four to eight single-spaced pages exclusive of supporting documentation. Data supporting the accomplishment of each objective are discussed in detail; summary commendations and recommendations are included. Teacher and evaluator then hold a conference, usually in April or May, to review the evaluation results and discuss areas of strength and deficiency.

Teachers are given a summary rating of "satisfactory" or "unsatisfactory" on the achievement of their objectives. When a teacher receives an unsatisfactory rating, a remediation plan is specified in detail, and the teacher must undergo evaluation in the following year rather than in the normal two-year cycle. A teacher who receives two successive ratings of unsatisfactory has his or her salary frozen until a satisfactory performance is displayed.

Evaluators have a variety of resources at their disposal when they construct a remediation plan. Department coordinators may work with teachers at the request of the principal; their expertise, especially in the teachers' subject area, often represents a valuable resource. District staff-development workshops serve as a targeted source of assistance. Evaluators may also draw on district resources to provide release time for teachers to observe effective colleagues and attend other workshops.

While teachers who receive a satisfactory evaluation are not formally evaluated in the following year, administrators are strongly urged to include recommendations for improvement in every teacher evaluation to serve as the basis for professional development activity for the following year.

STAFF DEVELOPMENT

Mountain View-Los Altos places a high premium on staff-development training. Superintendent Sakamoto believes it to be a necessary prerequisite for accountability. This commitment has been operationalized in two ways: the institution of a comprehensive program of staff-development training for teachers in the district, and the training of administrators in evaluation techniques.

For three years, beginning in 1981, teachers were offered a $500 salary increment for participating in district-wide staff-development efforts. "Equal Educational Opportunity in the Classroom," a program based on the instructional theories of Madeline Hunter, enjoyed an 80% participation rate. Several teachers and administrators received training in Los Angeles and then served as trainers for the rest of the professional staff. Several other programs have also been well attended. One workshop focused on the work of Jane Stallings and the effective use of instructional time;

another dealt with small-group instruction techniques. A $16,000 grant from the Packard Foundation, augmented by approximately $12,000 of local funds, financed these programs.

There is a direct link between evaluation results, training topics, and expectations that teachers demonstrate the effective teaching behaviors in their classrooms. Five different workshops, provided by district staff, are currently available to teachers, who now receive an hourly stipend for their participation. Analysis of teacher evaluation results from the previous year yielded the following topics for 1984–1985:

- Motivating and Expecting Higher Achievement
- Classroom Management and Discipline
- Teaching for Higher Level Thinking Through Interactive Instruction
- Testing for Higher Level Thinking
- Teaching for Different Learners

Praise for the workshops from teachers has been uniformly high:

> I learn something brand new in every workshop. What's most valuable . . . is hearing what's been successful for other people and simply seeing the fact that . . . other people are also groping for the same kinds of solutions.

One teacher, for whom participation in several workshops was recommended as part of a remediation plan, believes that staff-development programs represent one of the best features of working in Mountain View-Los Altos:

> I find that talking with other teachers so that they become a source of new ideas is probably more critical than anything else in helping [me] improve. I think the workshops provide a vehicle for that exchange.

Teachers consistently point not only to the process but also to the content of workshops as a source of professional stimulation. This positive response is a marked contrast to teachers' district-wide staff development in many school systems.

TRAINING OF ADMINISTRATORS

A second means to improve evaluation practice is through the training of administrators. For the past eight years, week-long summer workshops have focused on improving administrators' evaluation skills and on bringing consistency to the quality of teacher evaluation. Rather than focusing on a clinical supervision model, training methods attempt to improve the ability of administrators to gather objective information on teacher performance and to assess evidence of goal achievement. The rationale from one administrative workshop stated:

> Priority in evaluation procedures is on specificity and objectivity; that is, all parties to the process should know what is being communicated, observations and recommendations should be specific and realistic, and personal biases should be minimized. The completed evaluation packet should represent a valid documentation of the teacher's overall performance.

Evaluative skills are developed in several ways. Administrators observe videotapes of lessons, and their documentation skills are critiqued by their colleagues. Attorneys, serving as consultants, provide feedback on past evaluation reports, emphasizing the improvement of these documents as sources of evidence in administrative dismissal hearings.

Administrators agree unanimously on the value of district training efforts. The following comments of one building administrator are representative:

> I think reviewing the evaluations of past administrators has really helped me a lot in evaluating teachers. . . . For example, we discovered that we were all writing up the results of the students survey quite differently from school to school. We've also tried to talk about what you look for when you walk into a classroom.

By the same token, however, some administrators expressed some concern over the "legalistic focus" of the workshops. For example, these feelings were expressed by one administrator whose evaluative skill was praised by one of the department coordinators in his school:

> The focus [of evaluation] is on documenting things that stand up in court rather than letting teachers know what kind of job they are doing. . . . In fact, we were told by one legal consultant to be very careful about using positive comments because this can have an adverse effect in court and actually be used against us. This legalistic approach to evaluation has rubbed off. It's created a very negative morale situation in the district.

The pressure to excel, an adversarial relationship between district administrator and the teachers' union, and the development of a rigorous evaluation scheme have been responsible for several years of conflict between teachers and administrators and mixed responses to the evaluation system.

Progress to Date

Mountain View-Los Altos' evaluation system has been effective in holding teachers accountable for minimum performance levels. Over the past eight years, twenty-nine unsatisfactory evaluations have been given to a total of eighteen district teachers, representing approximately 7% of the workforce. Ten of these individuals voluntarily resigned. The remainder followed remediation plans and earned satisfactory ratings on subsequent evaluations. During 1984–1985, two unsatisfactory ratings were given. One teacher's salary has just been frozen as a result of two consecutive unsatisfactory evaluations.

The evaluation process applies the concept of accountability to teachers of all effectiveness levels, not just the minimally satisfactory. Professional incentives to excel in the presence of peers provide an external "nudge" which teachers believe to be important to maintain their effectiveness.

Asked whether poor teachers still exist in Mountain View-Los Altos, many teachers and administrators respond with their own question: "What do you mean by poor?" Expectations are extremely high in this district for teacher performance. According to one building administrator:

> In this district, we see the average teacher as someone who needs improvement. Here, in Los Altos, satisfactory just isn't good enough. . . . The Superintendent here makes it very clear that we want only the very best teachers in this district.

Some teachers embrace accountability goals vigorously. The following comment from one teacher who had just received a satisfactory evaluation is illustrative:

> The view that teachers are professionals and shouldn't be subject to administrators who inspect them is [hogwash]. We need people to come in and check on us just like anybody else. As long as it is done in a positive and constructive manner, all it can do is benefit education.

Another teacher says:

> I was scrutinized, but it was not a negative experience. This year, [my evaluator] spent a great deal of time on my evaluation, he attended to detail, he cared, and approached the task with thoughtfulness, and it was very accurate. . . . He had nothing but praise . . . and I really needed the strokes.

A veteran of twenty-three years states:

> I had the best evaluation experience ever this year. It was totally thorough; it was fair; and it was very positive . . . [my evaluator] respected my integrity as a teacher.

For some teachers, evaluation is not a salient part of their job; for others, it means "playing the game the way administrators like us to play it." As one young math teacher comments:

> I have to admit that I am fairly apathetic about evaluation. Mine have always been OK, so it really isn't that much of an issue for me.

A third group of teachers have strong negative feelings, believing that evaluation is used as a punitive measure. Indeed, every teacher who has positive feelings about his or her evaluation experience is also quick to point out that there were other teachers who feel differently. Some believe that older teachers are treated more critically than others. Addressing this point at the close of the 1984 school year, the outgoing president of the DTA sent a letter to the board of trustees on the negative impact of the district's evaluation policy on teachers. He argued, in particular, that the district's aggressive evaluation policies placed teachers under such stress that serious health problems resulted.

Certainly the legalistic emphasis of the evaluation process, while attempting to set a neutral tone, has been responsible for some of the teachers' negative reactions. One high-school principal comments:

> [It] has gotten much more impersonal, objective and lengthy because of the need for a solid foundation and a documentation of evidence of a teacher's weaknesses.

It is apparent that instituting a new evaluation system can be stressful for veteran teachers accustomed to other means. As one sympathetic administrator says, "I guess that a lot of the dissatisfaction that we see in the district at this time is because we had to start sometime and we caught a lot of teachers off guard in the middle of their careers."

Some teachers feel that those with reputations for good teaching have had different, less-stringent criteria applied to them in the past. One teacher of nineteen years' tenure, who received an unsatisfactory rating, feels he has been singled out, despite the fact that he improved greatly during the year:

> You are put in a certain mold and stuck there no matter what happens. I feel that last year I could have been observed any time, and when I was observed, I'd have to pitch a perfect inning just to get rated satisfactory, whereas other teachers could just coast along. It is just not necessary to do this "unsatisfactory" stuff to force a person to improve.

Teachers have complained that inconsistencies exist in the way in which evaluations were conducted from school to school and evaluator to evaluator. One high-school English teacher states:

> I really believe [that there is a need to standardize the way that evaluations are conducted]. They are very different. One person will be very casual and then the other will want every single handout that you have given for the entire year. One will spend an hour in a conference with you and the other won't even conference with you at all or conference with you in the hallway while you are walking to class or only spend ten minutes. There is a great disparity from evaluator to evaluator.

One assistant principal admits:

> I realize that I don't really deal with each teacher in exactly the same way. How I weight the various sources of information and how I construct the final evaluation really varies from teacher to teacher.

While administrators believe that the student survey provides invaluable information and should be retained, teachers agree on its elimination. The following represent the range of teachers' comments:

It causes such wide-spread discomfort, I wonder if it's worth it. Now I ask, are students really qualified to make the judgments we're asking them to make?

I'm torn [about the student survey]. In one way, it's very good, but I can see some students who don't take it seriously enough. Fortunately, it is not the only basis for judgment.

Superintendent Sakamoto believes that student surveys are "the strong point of our evaluation system in this district" and that administrators appear to place a high value on them. Says one high-school principal:

What the student results do is validate the rest of the evaluations. Some questions on the student questionnaire are extremely important. For example, the one about "the teacher returns student work promptly with helpful comments." I take special note of this question. I think that this is a big point and it's an ethical point for the teachers. It's an obligation to return work and provide feedback to students. Student-teacher relations, this is another question that I focus on. Only the students can really answer the question and know whether or not the relations are good.

Assistant superintendent Robert Madgic agrees:

I think it is really difficult to do an evaluation of a teacher without this input. Some teachers are just great performers during classroom observations. I think our focus has been to involve students as clients of the teacher's work. It reveals things that otherwise would not be revealed during the evaluation process. We eliminate some of the haphazardness that characterizes evaluations in other districts.

Union officials now believe that many of the inconsistencies in past evaluation practices have been rectified by administrators in the past few years. Continual monitoring and adjustment of evaluation practices and procedures in recent years has markedly reduced the number of teacher complaints. A recent survey revealed that 95% of all district teachers felt that their most recent evaluation was conducted fairly and objectively. The comments below suggest that when they experience the positive benefits of careful evaluation, their perceptions of fairness increase:

I have to admit that I was very concerned [about my evaluation] this year. The principal and I had some major disagreements when I first came to this school . . . and there were lots of rumours around that said I had a lot to worry about. . . . [Instead], I had a very positive experience with him this year. . . . His observation notes were very extensive and there was lots for me to discuss and his analysis took into account both my strengths and my weaknesses in a very balanced approach.

Another teacher comments:

As a teacher with a good reputation, I'm not sure [not having an evaluation system] would make that much difference except that if you're a person with high standards, you need to have a pat on your back now and then. Without evaluation, I would get very few strokes on my performance and getting these strokes helps me be a better teacher and helps me put these things into perspective. This year in particular was a tough year and the positive strokes really helped me. In fact I even went and discussed things with my evaluator in other classes than the ones that he was actually evaluating me on. I trusted him enough to share my vulnerabilities so that I could improve.

Though several teachers have received unsatisfactory ratings in the current year, union officials do not anticipate any grievances to result because of unfair practices. The president of the District Teachers' Association stated:

I don't think there are any major problems [with evaluation]. I think things have changed over the years and evolved. We have less complaints about evaluation this year than we did last year, so hopefully things are improving.

Administrators have taken specific steps in recent years to address problems with the evaluation system. The program is continually monitored and feedback elicited in attempts to improve it. According to Dr. Madgic:

We constantly try to focus the administrator's attention on evaluation. We point out problems of evaluation at principals' meetings. Evaluation is a topic at every one of those meetings, which occur once a week. We've emphasized evaluation every summer for the last eight summers in our administrative workshops in an effort to point out the problems with the process.

Madgic also concedes that

One problem that we have had in the past is that we haven't had well established criteria for teaching effectiveness that were widely shared and published for all to see. We expect to have this in place by the next school year. . . . Now we're attempting to make the criteria that we're using more explicit.

Administrators believe that the large amount of their time (an average of 20–25%) spent on evaluation is well worth it. Every administrator interviewed has identified evaluation as the number one job priority. While one assistant principal states that time spent on evaluation is "increasing all the time. And now I think we're just about saturated," most administrators express a desire to be given additional time to attend to evaluations even more closely.

Taken together, the responses of teachers and administrators in the district present a complex picture. Some teachers view evaluation as a force for professional improvement, a mechanism for formal recognition, and a tool for maintaining effectiveness. Others see it as a form of administrative harassment. Teachers' opinions seem to depend on their own most recent evaluation experience: variations in the quality of evaluations across evaluators seem to yield a wide range of opinion regarding evaluation's value.

In general, however, patience and persistence have paid off, and teachers' impressions of the evaluation process are increasingly positive. Several teachers who received an unsatisfactory evaluation in the previous year state that while the evaluation process produced a great deal of anxiety, it proved to be an effective means for improvement. According to one teacher with over seventeen years of experience:

There is no doubt in my mind that evaluation does help teachers improve. The workshops, the suggestions from the principal, materials they make available to help you—all these are good . . . there is certainly a lot of assistance in this district. I think it is sort of hand and glove—they provide you help and then they evaluate you on what you have learned and offer recommendations for improvement.

Another teacher comments:

[The principal] was very clear in stating his expectations, in recording observations, and making inferences clear. Even if they weren't all complimentary, I could see that the process is fair. Evaluation is good—it makes you grow. After [so many] years, you do get in a groove. I feel as though I really benefitted professionally this year.

This is from a teacher with over twenty years of experience:

Evaluation makes you sit down to think about what is really happening in your class. You say to yourself, "What am I doing?" Rarely do we have an opportunity in this profession to get introspective. But this process makes this introspection happen. . . . The real value of the process is it makes you think.

According to one veteran:

I believe what we have here is a good process. I'm proud to be part of this system and part of this evaluation process. I have always seen evaluation as being a helping relationship and I've always started the process every year with the idea of helping the teacher to improve by pinpointing areas that they can focus on.

THE MORAGA SCHOOL DISTRICT
TEACHER EVALUATION SYSTEM

[The Superintendent] tackled this in sections. She always accomplished things in steps. For example, she figured it would take three years to get all teachers through the program. She had to sell it to the teachers and the teachers eventually realized that they could be as good as the outsiders that first presented it to them. . . . So what has started is a breaking down of walls that isolate the teachers and puts them in reactive mode. Now the word is that everybody can be a better teacher. The parents have softened a bit, too. They have actually seen what the program can do because the teachers put on a show-and-tell and the board meeting demonstrating the process. Now it has gotten through the grapevine. We don't need a postal service here. If we can convince the key parents and educate them, they carry the ball. (Moraga School District board member.)

Moraga is a small bedroom community nestled in the hills on the east side of the San Francisco Bay. Moraga's school district is small, comprised of two elementary schools and one junior high that together serve approximately 1,400 students.

Moraga is an affluent community. Housing prices average well above the already-inflated Bay Area market. In the past several years, couples with young children have been increasingly unable to afford to live there, and the population of school-aged children has steadily declined. As a result, the school board was forced to close one of its schools two years ago and to lay off several teachers. Declining enrollments are a perpetual concern, and the layoffs of young, talented, and energetic teachers have been a frustrating experience for everyone in the district.

The vast majority of Moraga parents hold white-collar professional jobs in Oakland or San Francisco and maintain high expectations for their children and their school system. They play an active role in their childrens' education. A foundation set up by the district to raise funds to supplement state appropriations recently raised over $70,000 through a direct phone campaign. One elementary school's parents' club's fundraisers provided over $20,000 for the school to operate special programs. Another elementary school has over 150 parent volunteers who regularly work with students in the classroom. Every educator interviewed named parent support and involvement as the best part of working in the Moraga school district.

There are times, however, when the high level of parent participation becomes a problem for teachers and administrators. Over half of the teachers, especially at the elementary level, mention excessive and intrusive parent involvement as a problem. As one teacher states:

> The counter to bright, motivated, students is [assertive] parents. We pay for it. Kids like to learn, but there is lots of parent input that we don't want.

District administrators see one of their major roles as mediating between parents and the school. One principal notes:

> I need to be a facilitator between parents and the teachers. This is a powerful community, and parents often go straight to the top. Thus, I try to teach political skills to my staff.

This fine line between parent support and parent intrusion is something of which board members, administrators, and teachers are keenly aware. Parents maintain firm control over district finances through the school board and local fund-raising efforts. Their active classroom involvement allows them to closely monitor teacher performance, and complaints are prompt when they are unhappy.

Prior to the arrival of the current superintendent, Dr. Judith Glickman, teacher evaluation practices in Moraga were as problematic as those found in most of this country's school districts. According to teachers, evaluation was characterized by brief and infrequent observations and a lack of follow-up. Further, many teachers could not name the five broad areas in which they were evaluated, believing that these categories existed for the administration's benefit, not theirs. One teacher comments, "I guess the year end form can't be very important if I can't even remember what's on it." The statement of another teacher sums up the feeling of the staff regarding past practices: "It wouldn't make any difference to me if evaluation never happened."

Former evaluation methods achieved neither accountability nor improvement objectives for Moraga. Principals felt they lacked the proper training and support to do valid evaluations. Most teachers saw the evaluation process as inconsequential to their classroom performance. However, teachers also acknowledged that the existence of a partially merit-based salary schedule sometimes transformed evaluations into an unfair, politicized, and punitive tool.

Merit Pay

The collective bargaining agreement between teachers and the board of education in Moraga contains a unique provision. Referred to as the eighteenth and twenty-third step provision, it denies a salary increment of $750 at the end of the seventeenth and twenty-second year of service if a teacher does not receive at least a "good" composite year-end rating or receives an unsatisfactory rating in any of the subcategories. No appeal is allowed, but teachers must be given a year's advance notice if it seems likely that the salary increment will be denied.

According to school board members, this is one of the only mechanisms to let teachers know that their performance is unacceptable. Teachers, on the other hand, feel it is unfair to wait so long to let them know the administration has serious doubts about their ability to perform acceptably:

> Why do they wait until the eighteenth year to tell you you stink? What's worse, everybody in the district knows it if you don't get it. It only creates

dissent and hard feelings. It is not a reward, it's a punishment. It has not helped any poor teacher improve.

Principals also have strong negative feelings regarding this aspect of the evaluation process:

> I don't believe [the eighteenth and twenty-third step provision] does any-thing it was intended to do. It forces me to make judgments I can't make in a valid way. It is a bribe and highly politicized. It is demeaning. It forces teachers to grovel. It has no place in an open organization.

There may have been incidents in the past where parent complaints and pressure on the school board and superintendent resulted in the denial of the salary increment. The feeling that arbitrary decisions of this kind are being made "upstairs" has surfaced as a tremendous distrust of district management. Several respondents related the story of a teacher who was told he would receive the salary increment, only to be denied it when the principal returned from a meeting at the central office. To this end, one respondent reported:

> There has been a long history of poor relations with the Superintendent [prior to Glickman]. Principals, in the past, were seen as victims, caught in the middle. The Superintendent would decide who would get dinged and expected the principal to legitimate and communicate this decision to the teacher.

Whether or not these stories are entirely true, teachers' beliefs in them demonstrate the lack of trust that existed between teachers and district management prior to the arrival of the current superintendent. Seventy-five percent of the respondents specifically mention distrust of the central administration in the past as an obstacle to improvement. As one board member puts it, "Before, the teachers thought the board didn't like them. The attitude was that we were out to get them."

Another board member captures the fractionated and adversarial nature of the teacher-administrator-school board relations prior to the arrival of the current superintendent:

> Parents wanted perfect teachers for their kids. They wanted to get rid of the bad teachers. The teachers circled their wagons and banded together in reaction to parent criticism. . . . The Superintendent tried to zero in

to get rid of the bad teachers. His message was "I'll get you if you slip up." This pushed the teachers closer together, while the principals got stuck in the middle of the entire process.

As district enrollments declined and it became clear that some teachers would be laid off, the community pressure to eliminate less than satisfactory teachers increased. Trust levels within the district reached an all-time low. This was the situation which faced Judith Glickman as she took the job of Superintendent of the Moraga School District.

Establishing Trust

Now we don't talk about good or bad teachers. Instead, we talk about skills. Teachers, parents, and administrators work together more now. We work on goals instead of personalities. Now, we try to build the best house, not determine who the best subcontractors are.

This comment, made by a board member and guardedly shared by most of Moraga's teachers, reflects the changes that have come about in the last several years under Glickman's leadership. The school board wanted to hire a superintendent who could serve as an instructional leader for the district, one who would improve both staff and curriculum. According to Glickman, this was what attracted her to the district:

I sensed in my interview that [the board] wanted a cohesive, long-term plan for staff development and curriculum improvement. This was up front from the beginning. They knew they wanted results, but didn't know how to get them.

This match between the board's educational philosophy and the superintendent's professional values set the stage for major changes in the form and focus of district management in Moraga.

Glickman took several important steps to address the lack of trust between teachers and central administration. She held a personal conference with every district teacher to discuss their educational philosophy and professional goals. A management team composed of central-office staff and building principals was formed in an effort to increase involvement in district decision making. The superintendent now spends two days each month in classrooms observing teachers. A formal goal-setting process was instituted. District goals became translated into goals for the superintendent, which became goals for principals and finally teachers. Through these efforts, the superintendent attempted to bring an openness and clarity to district management that had not previously existed.

Institutionalizing trust in any organization is difficult. Glickman's task, to deal with several incompetent teachers, only exacerbated the problem. Yet the principals, who had daily contact with the superintendent, warmed quickly to her open style. The following comment is representative of all district administrators:

> This is the best management relationship I have ever worked under. [Dr. Glickman] delegates responsibility so that I feel part of a team. I am valued, heard, and my concerns are addressed. I feel my school is a part of the district and aims at district goals. I trust her and share her vision.

Teachers have a mixed response to Glickman's management style. The following represents the range of teacher comments:

> She has strong opinions and plans. She takes input and makes strong decisions—but the intput means little.

> Compared to the former one, she is a breath of fresh air. She has a clear direction and leads.

> She is trying to make a two-way street—she asks for input.

> She is professional and polite. She plays no favorites. But she is like the tundra in the summertime—go down a foot and she's as hard as a rock.

Two teachers recall a meeting regarding education foundation priorities to support their respective positions. In this faculty meeting, the principal had asked teachers to break into groups and brainstorm on possible uses for extra funds. These ideas, along with those developed by other schools, would be used by the school board to set priorities for the coming year. While one teacher felt this represented an excellent example of the input teachers had in the district, the other saw it as the administration's attempt to provide the "appearance" of input. According to this teacher, "The decision had already been made."

Past experience has conditioned Moraga teachers to be guarded in their trust of district administrators. Though no teacher can cite an example where the superintendent has betrayed a teacher's trust, most remain wary.

Evaluation Strategies

From its inception, Glickman's district management team believed in the necessity of placing administrators and teachers on common ground to ensure the effectiveness of a new evaluation process. Like Mountain View-Los Altos, the determined course of action for Moraga consisted of improving district staff development activities and intensive administrative training in clinical supervision skills. According to Glickman:

> Staff development articulates what is appropriate instruction. . . . Formal evaluation serves to get someone's attention . . . and can be used to prove fairness to other teachers. Clarity and openness are the key to success.

The management team agreed to adopt a staff-development program developed by another district and based on the work of Madeline Hunter. The entire management team and seven teachers received training which focused on clearly identified instructional skills drawn from research on effective teaching. These individuals then became trainers for the rest of the teachers in the district. The district paid teachers to attend a three-day summer workshop for two consecutive years. Though teachers attended voluntarily, the district informed them that this training would serve as the focus for teacher evaluation in the future. To date, 97% of Moraga's teachers have participated in the training, called Elements of Effective Instruction (EEI).

While teachers participated in EEI training, district administrators received clinical supervision skills using the model of Richard Mannatt. An administrator from another district was retained to serve as a consultant to assist principals in applying EEI principles to their classroom observations. Principals were unanimous in their praise of the consultant's efforts, and he, in return, felt confident that their evaluative skills had improved considerably.

The investment of district resources and administrative time and energy on training has had an additional effect: it symbolizes a shift in district priorities. Glickman now expected principals to spend time with teachers in the classroom. Glickman models this behavior herself, reads every evaluation and observation report prepared by administrators, and offers feedback when appropriate. Principals know that evaluating teachers is a valued activity and believe the superintendent holds them strictly accountable for these duties. As one principal puts it:

[The superintendent] makes her priorities very clear. She really knows what goes on in every school building. But evaluation tops her list. She holds me accountable and I take extra care with evaluation as a result.

The common language for teachers and administrators provided by EEI, coupled with clinical supervision training, have produced a number of changes in the process principals use to evaluate teachers:

- Preobservation conferences with the teacher are held to negotiate specific areas of focus are now standard practice.
- Principals observe and comment on specific training skills rather than global, unobservable criteria.
- Principals now have complete autonomy in determining the improvement needs of individual teachers on the staff.
- Written script-tapes accompany all formal observations.
- Principals carefully plan post-observation conferences. They share their recommendations, which become the focus of the next observation.
- Principals now conduct three to four formal observations during a teacher's evaluation year, rather than the one or two that occurred in the past.

Teachers' reactions to the EEI program are generally positive, but their reasons differ considerably. One teacher mentions that the workshops are boring but also comments that, given the future plans to link the EEI training to the evaluation process, it is most appropriate for this purpose:

> They told you things that you already knew—things that you were already doing. There was nothing exciting for me. . . . EEI was "make work." . . . To evaluate [using] EEI . . . makes things clear. Other kinds of inservice wouldn't be appropriate. EEI is better. . . . It is good, clear, and simple.

The majority of teachers believe that participation in the EEI training was a "validating" experience. They find it reassuring that research on teaching has identified techniques that they already used in the classroom:

> I found [EEI] to be very useful. I realized that there were so many fabulous teachers in this district. It validated what I'm already doing—it was reinforcing for me.

Teachers point to the value of positive reinforcement. They feel that the district has acknowledged the importance of the job they do by spending money outside of the normal school year to increase instructional skills—a sharp contrast to the fiscal conservatism of the past. The presence of Moraga teachers as trainers has also had symbolic meaning for some.

Teachers identify several additional effects of the EEI training. Over half of the teachers report that they actually have changed the way they teach day to day as a result of the training. Examples of concepts that Moraga teachers have put into practice include checking for understanding from one activity to the next; effective use of instructional time; changes in lesson planning; the use of questioning techniques to encourage higher level thinking skills, even in kindergarten; and increased use of guided practice.

Other teachers find value in EEI's impact on collegial relations. The following comment suggests the effect of lowering of barriers that isolate teachers from one another:

> It brought the teaching staff together, like we used to be a long time ago. We rarely do things together anymore. It helped to strengthen ties. It crossed lines; even the administration was there. It was a cohesive experience and made us feel like a family again.

Several teachers mention that conversations in the faculty lounge now focus on instructional matters to a greater extent than before. In fact, the entire bulletin board in the teacher's lounge at one school is devoted to "The Ultimate Five-Step Lesson Plan," a theme from the EEI program.

To the extent that information collected during classroom obser- vations results in discussion and problem-solving between teachers and administrators, EEI has set the stage for a realignment of influence spheres that prevented this dialogue from occurring in the past. One mentor teacher in the district states:

> The principal has made [evaluation] an ongoing process this year. . . . There is no territoriality—that is, I don't see my room as mine alone. He is aware, he knows, he sees, and this leads to fairness and reliability. I value his feedback.

Administrators react uniformly and positively to the EEI program. They feel empowered as a result of the training. Though teachers retain some autonomy in monitoring and changing their own teaching, EEI has provided a basis for dialogue between administrators and teachers which previously did not exist. One administrator described the impact this way:

> [EEI provided] a common way of looking at teaching—a vocabulary. [Teachers and administrators] can now talk about instruction at faculty meetings. For example, we just finished discussing how one teaches independence—we could all share and talk because we had a common grounding.

Teacher accountability is not reserved for the incompetent; effective teachers want to know how they are doing and the new attention to evaluation in Moraga provides them with an important source of recognition and validation that was lacking in the past. An elementary teacher states:

> I want the administration to be interested in what I am doing. . . . It gives a teacher a sense of importance when [an administrator] feels that what they're doing is important enough for him to drop in to see how it is going.

Changes in the evaluation process are welcomed by teachers and principals alike for two reasons. First, they provide clarity in the process, and the increased emphasis on documentation contributes to the fairness of the entire system. The teachers' organization president comments:

> I'm glad to see a formalized and thorough evaluation. Writing things down is good—it is there in black and white. Not only the administrators, but the teachers, too, have something to refer to.

This comment is reinforced by another teacher with over twenty years of experience:

> Tying evaluation to the Elements of Effective Instruction has given us a scaffolding to hang evaluations on. It prevents misunderstandings.

One example illustrates the new degree of clarity in Moraga's evaluation system. Prior to Dr. Glickman's arrival, the board had denied a salary increment to a particular teacher because of complaints about his performance by parents. Last year this teacher received the increase: the documentation of his improvement provided convincing evidence that he deserved an acceptable rating. The evaluation system helped this teacher improve, and it also provided evidence to mediate parent complaints.

A second reason teachers and administrators welcome the changes in the evaluation process is that they believe it can support teachers in their efforts to improve and maintain their classroom effectiveness. Preobservation conferences allow teachers some degree of control over the focus of their observations; script-tapes (verbatim transcripts of the lesson) serve as excellent sources of feedback to the teacher; and follow-up from observation to observation keeps attention focused on desired changes. According to a teacher in the intermediate school:

> [Evaluation] really has made me more conscious about how to do things in my classroom. I am much more conscious overall about my practice and I think about my lessons more systematically.

None of Moraga's teachers have mentioned feeling constrained in any way by the evaluation process or its focus on the principles of effective instruction as stated in the EEI program. Though the potential for standardization exists, teachers appear to trust their principals to allow them the flexibility to innovate.

Progress to Date

The reports of teachers and administrators illustrate that the steps taken to date—establishing priorities, building trust, developing a common language, training evaluators, EEI training—represent necessary but not yet sufficient conditions for producing instructional improvement. Teachers acknowledge that evaluation has the potential to serve as a force for professional improvement but that limitations of time, resources, and training for both teachers and administrators have limited the effectiveness of the evaluation process.

District administrators are clear that they are only part way through the process of developing and establishing the evaluation system. Moraga has thus far focused its evaluation reforms on the evaluation *process*, not on specific forms or instruments. There are some advantages to this: because principals have no forms on which to write up their formal observations, they avoid many of the problems inherent with using rating scales. At the same time, current evaluation methods are much more formalized than past practices. Feedback must be rigorously documented, and principals spend about twice as much time on evaluation than they did prior to the new system. The year-end evaluation form, a checklist that has been in use for many years, is still employed, but principals can now support their ratings with evidence gathered during classroom observations. This form is not consistent, however, with the content of recent training efforts in the district, and this has caused some problems. One principal describes the situation this way:

> The end-of-the-year form is a dinosaur. It's this way because of the previous posture of the district toward teachers. We will change it, but now the form doesn't fit the [instructional] model we use. But things take time, and I feel we are on target at this point in time.

The comments of this veteran teacher reflect the feelings of most of the teachers we spoke with:

> Getting rid of the end-of-the-year form is key [to further improving the evaluation system]. Currently, it is a waste of time. Until then, I'm sure the principals see evaluation as a nightmare.

Teachers and administrators are currently negotiating a new year-end evaluation form and plan to have a new one in place by the end of the current year.

As an accountability tool, revisions in the evaluation process have paid off. Over the last three years, ten percent of Moraga's teachers have been induced to resign as a direct result of evaluative feedback. Further, none of the teachers interviewed in this study indicated that the district acted unfairly in these cases. Instead, they saw these departures as a response to classroom performance that fall short of clearly, openly communicated criteria.

The negative reactions of teachers and administrators regarding the eighteenth and twenty-third step merit-plan provision have already been described. Superintendent Glickman acknowledges that this feature is not consistent with her overall management philosophy and has promised to come up with an acceptable alternative. Until then, in the words of one teacher, "it remains a vestige of past management practices."

Follow-up to the EEI program has not yet materialized as the super-intendent would have liked. Though each principal describes follow-up activities conducted with their staff during regularly scheduled faculty meetings, many teachers claim that a lack of follow-up is a major weakness of the program. One intermediate-school teacher puts it bluntly:

> With EEI, the district has dropped the ball because they didn't bring the teachers together again until January. By then, much of the enthuasiasm was gone for all participants. There was just no follow-up.

The administration has encouraged teachers to conduct collegial observations or videotape their lessons, but few teachers have done this. Respondents mention a lack of time and lack of training in observation and evaluation skills as major impediments to participating in these activities. According to one administrator:

> I have the clinical supervision part. The teachers don't. They don't understand the whole process. Collegial observations are not working because teachers don't know what to do.

Another obstacle Moraga must overcome involves addressing the issue of administrator time and resources to support evaluation efforts. Unlike Santa Clara and Mountain View-Los Altos, Moraga receives no special resources to assist in addressing teachers' improvement needs and has had difficulty finding the time to implement the new evaluation process consistently with every teacher on their staff. As in Santa Clara and Mountain View-Los Altos, they have chosen to focus their limited time and energy on those teachers they believe are most in need of attention.

Several examples illustrate the effects of this uneven attention to evaluation from teacher to teacher. One teacher, who reports receiving a great deal of assistance from the principal throughout the formal evaluation process, believes that this attention has caused considerable improvement in his teaching. But another respondent, identified by her principal as an excellent teacher, was quite upset because her evaluator could not provide her with the help and assistance she requested because he was too busy and lacked the training. "I was furious," she states. "Why couldn't he help? He could have helped, but his priority was not really helping."

Another teacher reports that her observations in the previous year were "informal because the principal was working on developing his own skills." Some teachers report that they have observed no change at all in the evaluation process over the last several years. But these all represent comments on a process that is still evolving.

In general, however, Moraga teachers feel that the process is more fair and reliable than in the past because principals are in their classrooms more often, have more skills, and are more confident and open in their feedback. As one teacher puts it, "The principal has made evaluation an ongoing process this year. Now, there is no territoriality; I don't see my room as mine alone."

One teacher who has taught in the district for over twenty years describes the current relationship between teachers and administrators in the district using the following metaphor:

> Schools are like a dark room with a large globe in the center. All the actors—teachers, administrators, board members, and parents—stand around the globe with flashlights. If we all use our flashlights and shine them on the globe, we light the place up and we all can see. But if only one or two flashlights are on, we grope in the dark.
>
> So often, only the management uses their flashlights to try and find the way, and they never ask us to use ours. We've just begun to take advantage of one another's flashlights here in Moraga.

THE CHARLOTTE–MECKLENBURG SCHOOLS TEACHER EVALUATION SYSTEM

> This is a total program and this is only the start. In the beginning we have to ask teachers to demonstrate that they have the ability to display the science of teaching. Then, later in their careers, they can build upon this and develop the art of teaching, taking advantage of their own creativity and individual needs. . . . Our goal is to build in flexibility to the instruction that teachers bring to kids, and we want teachers to build on a base of effective teaching. . . . I think this is the strength of the program. (Director of Career Development, Charlotte-Mecklenburg Schools.)

The Charlotte-Mecklenburg Schools, a large urban public school district, serves approximately 72,000 students living in the city of Charlotte, North Carolina, and surrounding Mecklenburg County. In 1982, it ranked as the thirtieth largest school system in the U.S. Though its student body has declined in the past decade from a high of 90,000, enrollments are relatively stable at this time. Forty percent of the student population is minority.

The school district employs 4,200 teachers; the average length of service is fifteen years for secondary teachers and twelve years for elementary teachers. As a result of a modest enrollment increase, teacher retirements, and normal turnover, the district projects a need to hire 1,600 to 2,000 teachers over the next five years.

The school district's average per-pupil expenditure of $2,745 is the second highest in the state. There is a state salary schedule for teachers, but school districts may supplement it if they wish. Local district expenditures, which must be approved by the Mecklenburg County Commissioners, contribute 33% of the total operating budget. Before the implementation of the Career Development Program in Charlotte, teachers' salaries ranged from $16,738 to $27,000, with an average of $22,720. Salaries for teachers under the Career Development Program range from $16,738 to $34,810.

There is no collective bargaining law in North Carolina, but teacher evaluation procedures are specified by the state. There are three active professional organizations for district teachers: one is an NEA affiliate, another an American Federation of Teachers (AFT) affiliate, and the third is a local association called the Classroom Teachers Association. Representatives of all three associations believe that the working relationship between them and the superintendent could not be improved upon. Even in the absence of collective bargaining, these associations provide a great amount of input in the formulation of district policy. Such was the case with career development. As one union representative puts it:

> My organization's relationship [with the Superintendent] is as good as it can be. It is very productive. I would say this about no other Superintendent, but I believe that collective bargaining could actually get in the way and would inhibit the relationship that we have right now.

The Career Development Program

Teacher evaluation in Charlotte operates within the context of the Career Development Program. Three important contextual factors directly contributed to the district's success in planning and implementing this comprehensive program: (1) the impetus provided by impending state actions regarding a state-wide merit-pay plan for teachers; (2) the presence of technical expertise, most notably the managerial skills of superintendent Jay Robinson and the theoretical knowledge of special assistant to the superintendent Phillip Schlecty; and (3) a strong commitment to staff development, emphasizing instructional excellence.

The Career Development Program, with its emphasis on teacher evaluation, emerged in 1981 with the formation of a district-wide committee to study the prospects of instituting a merit-pay plan. Composed of representatives from colleges and universities, the business community, the board of education, PTA, presidents of the three local teacher organizations, and teachers and administrators, the committee concluded that there was no merit-pay system in current existence that would work for Charlotte. The following excerpt from their letter to the superintendent in December, 1981, portrays their sentiments:

> There is no existing system of merit pay in schools that can provide a model for CMS [Charlotte-Mecklenburg Schools]. Indeed, there is more evidence to support the assertion that merit pay has had harmful and disruptive effects than that it has had positive effects. In spite of these facts, there is strong evidence that some form of merit pay will be imposed on CMS and every other school system in the state in the near future. If CMS is to escape the negative consequences that are likely to flow from such a state mandated program, the system has two options: a) prepare a strong statement, based upon available evidence against merit pay and resist the imposition with logic and political power, or b) endeavor to capture the momentum created by the present state-wide concern with teacher evaluation and merit pay to create a comprehensive system of incentives and evaluation that is logical and that would work if it were implemented.

Confronted with these recommendations, the superintendent charged the committee with drafting the latter alternative. The prospect of a state-wide merit-pay program in the future provided the impetus for the planning of an alternative.

LEADERSHIP

Much of the credit for the district's accomplishments is attributed to superintendent Jay Robinson. His associates describe him as a "risk taker with a bias for action." His management approach creates an environment where innovation and creativity are not only likely but are expected. According to one administrator: ". . . accidental inventions more frequently occur in well-prepared labs. Charlotte's lab is well-prepared and ready to embrace invention."

The joint leadership of superintendent Jay Robinson and Phillip Schlechty enhanced the strengths each brought to the job. Schlechty brought his expertise on the shape of the teaching workforce and the sociology of organizations to guide the merit-pay committee through some difficult deliberations, and Robinson's open management style and political savvy helped to make the career development plan a reality. Their collaborative effort demonstrates a successful marriage between research, theory, and practice. Schlechty described their working relationship as follows:

> Jay, as a manager with a bias for action, and I, as a university professor with a bias for reflection, interacted quite well and modified each other in the process. I learned to act more quickly even if I didn't have all the information I wanted, and Jay learned to pause sometimes and wait before he acted. We met somewhere in the middle.

Schlechty has likened Charlotte's first year of the Career Development Program to "building an airplane while it is in flight."

STAFF DEVELOPMENT

The people of Charlotte take great pride in the progressive nature of their community. A history of creativity and innovation in approaching social problems dates back to the implementation of a model plan to desegregate the schools through busing in the early 1970s. Several teachers have indicated that they chose to teach in this district precisely because of its commitment to racial integration.

Experimentation and creativity have been evident in the district's commitment to staff development. A locally financed Teaching Learning Center, established in 1976, routinely serves 1,000 teachers a month. In the past three years every teacher and administrator, including the superintendent, has participated in a workshop series on effective teaching, a program which illustrates Madeline Hunter's lesson design and presentation principles. A Curriculum Research Center, a comprehensive collection of professional materials to stimulate innovation in curriculum design and teaching methods, is also available to the professional staff.

An entire school building has been converted into a staff development center. Classrooms and office space are used not only for a wide variety of staff development programs but also to house field-based degree programs for several universities and the Metrolina Education Consortium. Four trained psychologists also staff an employee assistance program.

The district considers individual teacher performance in terms of district capacities. For example, the assistant superintendent for personnel's response to a question on the effectiveness of district teachers and administrators is indicative of Charlotte-Mecklenburg's commitment to staff development. "That isn't an appropriate question," he replies. "Instead, you should be asking about our commitment to training. How outstanding [our people] are depends on how committed the district is to producing and training outstanding individuals."

Charlotte's Career Development Program exemplifies the district's willingness to experiment. The program grew out of a belief that attracting and retaining effective teachers would require a new career structure that incorporated fundamental changes in the way in which teachers are trained, evaluated, and rewarded. Most of the training resources already existed as part of the district's well-developed staff-development program. Career development has identified the most successful elements and coordinated them to improve teaching effectiveness. Administrators point out that the Career Development Program is typical of the district's pragmatic approach. Phillip Schlechty, a University of North Carolina professor who served as special assistant to the superintendent to plan and implement the Career Development Program, describes the district as "organizationally strong."

Charlotte-Mecklenburg has also acknowledged the importance of integrating training and evaluation. The staff-development office in the district coordinates all of the training for the variety of roles which take part in career development and teacher evaluation. The director of staff development works closely with the area program specialists to insure that teachers are supported in fulfilling the recommendations of the advisory-assistance teams responsible for their evaluation. As both the input to and consequences of the evaluation process, staff development is an integral part of professional life in this district.

Additional benefits to the melding together of staff-development training and evaluation are evident in Charlotte. Being targeted for special assistance is typically perceived as a sign of incompetence, a stigma which dissuades many administrators from recommending it for their teachers. The Career Development Program, in contrast, makes staff development a routine part of evaluation. Even career candidates can receive extensive assistance without triggering any negative responses from other staff. Provisional teachers are vigorously supported in their attempts to respond to evaluative feedback. One junior high-school provisional teacher who received some feedback on her teaching of writing offers the following example of the specific kinds of training which are possible:

> Because they have such a writing emphasis in the school and in the district, they are going to send me to observe a writing teacher in another school. It was the assistant principal for instruction who arranged this and got the sub to cover my classes. I really believe that I need this help and I am looking forward to it. . . . Any issue I need to address, the Assistant Principal for Instruction has helped me. She has been wonderful. I really haven't had any lack of resources.

The entire delivery system for district-wide staff development supports career development. A series of school-based workshops have been targeted to the needs of provisional teachers in one large high school. Such offerings never existed in the past. An assistant principal for instruction offered this description of how career development has utilized staff-development resources:

> We have provided specific assistance [to provisional teachers and career candidates] such as assertive discipline workshops and I'm not sure that some of these teachers would have been referred to them without having this evaluation system in place. For example, last year I didn't refer anyone to specific workshops in the district. This year, I've done it at least five times.

One example of the district's commitment to staff development is the presence of an assistant principal for instruction in every school. These ninety-four individuals, originally referred to as "coordinating teachers," are explicitly charged with conducting and managing staff-development and curriculum-development activities at individual school sites. At the area level they work directly with area program specialists as brokers of staff development and curricular resources for teachers.

Evaluation Strategies

The Merit Pay Committee, which provided some of the original impetus for the Career Development Program, had a strong belief in the importance of teacher evaluation. It held that the existing system contributed little to the district's ability to meet its goals of instructional excellence and that revision would be meaningless unless the district linked evaluation results to positive as well as negative sanctions. The district was thus prompted to make evaluation reform the linchpin of the new Career Development Program. The following excerpt from the committee's report reflects this stance:

> . . . performance evaluations that are not linked to positive rewards or to the potential of positive rewards are inherently punitive. Put directly, if positive evaluations are not used to enhance one's reputation or status, if positive evaluations are not used to make one eligible to accept new responsibilities and gain enriched job assignments, and if positive evaluations are not used to determine expanding career options, then the only evaluations that count are those that are negative. Unfortunately, the way schools are now organized, negative evaluations are the only evaluations that count since positive evaluations are not linked to any rewards that count.

A twenty-one-member ad-hoc committee was selected to design the specifics of the Career Development Program and the evaluation system. The district obtained a planning grant from the U.S. Department of Education to pay for the work of the committee and the salaries of six regional teachers to serve as liaisons between building teachers and the steering committee. School-level representatives were called together on a monthly basis for day-long meetings to exchange ideas with the steering committee. The Career Development Program and its teacher evaluation component are the result of the work of these committees over a twelve-month period. The impact of this approach on teachers' attitudes reveals itself in this comment from a veteran elementary-school teacher who is participating as a career candidate in the program:

> The crux of this program so far is teachers making decisions . . . I watched the planning process closely, and I just don't see how the whole developmental process could have had more teacher input. I say this even though some felt there wasn't enough, but I don't think that they're being reasonable.

The steering committee recommended that participation in the Career Development Program should be voluntary for all teachers hired by Charlotte-Mecklenburg prior to the 1984–1985 school year. This decision reduced the potential of anxiety for older teachers and allowed them to observe the mechanics of the evaluation process before making the decision to participate. It also precluded the possibility that implementation of this complex program would outstrip the capacity of the district's human and financial resources.

The steering committee devised a selection procedure for experienced teachers such that the initial pool of one hundred and fifty would reflect the district's ethnic balance. To be selected, a teacher not only had to volunteer but also had to be nominated by his or her principal or peers as an outstanding teacher. The district plans eventually to provide every experienced teacher the opportunity to enter the Career Development Program. Meanwhile, all new nontenured teachers are required under North Carolina law to participate in the new evaluation process.

New teachers begin as provisional teachers, advancing over a period of years to become career nominees, career candidates, and Career Level I, II, or III teachers, based on the results of their evaluations. Each new position involves additional responsibilities and increased pay. The district obtained a waiver of the state's teacher tenure law to allow for a post-ponement of the decision to grant tenure until the fourth-to-sixth year of a teacher's career, depending on progress in attaining the requisite skills. Career Level I status accompanies the awarding of tenure. Decisions to pursue Career Level II and III status are voluntary for all teachers.

Experienced Charlotte-Mecklenburg teachers who choose to partic-ipate in the Career Development Program skip the provisional and career nominee stages. They enter the process as career candidates and undergo an evaluation process adapted to reflect their participation in the program.

Three basic principles provide the basis for the new evaluation proc-ess. First, teachers function as managers and as such should be held accountable only for those results over which they have control. The basic evaluation tool is the Carolina Teaching Performance Assessment Scale (CTPAS), which is directly based on research on effective teaching. It measures teacher performance in five skill areas: (1) managing instruc-tional time, (2) managing student behavior, (3) presenting instruction, (4) monitoring instruction, and (5) obtaining instructional feedback. Adopting the CTPAS instrument saved district planners time and resources. Rather than viewing the state instrument as a constraint, they took advan-tage of the time, research, and validation that had gone into its construc-tion and focused their energy on other issues. As one administrator said, "[The CTPAS] is just common sense; there is really nothing wrong with it. . . . Like a preflight checklist, it is a necessary but not sufficient condition for effective teaching."

A second principle undergirding the evaluation process is that teaching is a developmental career. While competence in the skills identified in the effective teaching literature rests at the base of that developmental process, experienced teachers are expected to be able to grow beyond this point. Fourteen additional competencies form the basis for the evaluations of more experienced teachers:

1. To maintain mastery of the subject matter he or she is assigned to teach and to maintain technical expertise in his or her assigned area(s) of responsibility;
2. To assess and to monitor student performance in a manner consistent with the best available knowledge in the field of evaluation;
3. To provide effective management and instruction consistent with the best available knowledge in the field of teaching and learning;
4. To provide students with maximum access to resources in the school system and in the community;
5. To recognize and to respond positively, appropriately, and with concern to the needs of all students, including students from diverse cultural and ethnic backgrounds, the handicapped, and the gifted;
6. To establish high expectations for students performance and to provide motivation, management, instruction, guidance, and support to insure that students meet these expectations;
7. To communicate effectively with staff, parents, and students about his or her area of expertise or job assignment;
8. To participate in planning, implementing, and evaluating school programs;
9. To participate in and to support activities designed to enhance the school and to achieve its goals;
10. To serve as a role model for other teachers;
11. To participate in research and development activities to improve instruction, such as the creation and testing of alternative curriculum materials and strategies;
12. To engage in continuous self-evaluation and to alter his or her performance in response;
13. To participate in the evaluation process to determine if he or she is meeting the requirements for Career Level I status; and
14. To maintain an awareness of trends and issues addressed by professionals organizations and to become involved, when appropriate, in addressing those issues.

A final principle of the evaluation process is that evaluation cannot be conducted outside the context of human judgment. To insure quality, evaluations are conducted by a number of individuals who employ multiple and explicit criteria over a long period of time. Schlechty reveals this underlying philosophy:

> We did not approach evaluation as a legal and technical task; instead we approached it as a political and moral task. Issues of reliability are less important than issues of validity.

The primary responsibility for evaluation rests with school-level advisory/assistance teams. Team members consider it their professional responsibility to provide teachers with every bit of assistance necessary to succeed. No longer must an overburdened principal take sole responsibility for conducting observations and for providing professional support. As one principal states:

> In the past, any possibility that successful growth would occur in a teacher as a result of evaluation depended on a personal relationship that would exist between the principal and the teacher. The old system was a rela-tionship-based system—now we have a professionally based system. Now, we involve other people in the process.

Without exception, those teachers who were dissatisfied with the evaluation process are those who report receiving little support or guidance from their advisory/assistant teams. The majority of these teams, however, are rated highly. One enthusiastic teacher states:

> [The advisory/assistance team has] been my right arm. I couldn't have done what I've done without them. . . . My chairperson has contributed so much. I feel badly using those people free of charge. . . . Yesterday morning we had a meeting at 6:45 A.M.

The presence of system-wide observer/evaluators (O/Es) introduces an accountability factor that brings some degree of standardization throughout the district. Charlotte-Mecklenburg has largely overcome a problem that plagues teacher evaluation in many districts—the fact that a teacher's evaluation often varies with the evaluator's. The comments of one building principal echo the sentiments of administrators and teachers alike:

I believe the observer/evaluators are the key objective link that holds the whole system together. They measure how consistent the AA [advisory/ assistance] teams are across the district. . . . They also help to give the AA teams feedback. The O/Es provide a check for what these teams are doing. . . . We spend time comparing the O/E reports with our own and carefully try to explain any differences that exist.

Her comments are reinforced by this high-school career candidate:

I think that it's good that the observer/evaluators come in from the outside. They help make the system valid and keep bias from creeping in. . . . Holding people accountable is the beginning to bringing about improvement in the district.

The observer/evaluators take great pride in the care they give to their observations. Each hour-long observation takes an average of four hours to write up. Observer/evaluators see themselves as outsiders providing an objective "snapshot" of a given lesson as the key to the system's integrity:

We give data. We do not evaluate. [Though] we do place value when we circle a 1, 2, or 3, we don't have the power to make any final judgments and we believe this is the key to the success of the process. One of the reasons we have nine observations is to allow for a teacher to have a bad day.

Area and district-level review committees serve as a final check that the evaluation system is being implemented consistently with district goals, and this ongoing review is supported throughout the year by area administrators. According to one area superintendent:

I don't let [advisory/assistance teams] off the hook. I insist that the school-based committees arrive at a decision that they can justify. . . . I have my area program specialists work in the schools and meet with teams and teachers to make sure they understand what is expected of them.

PROVISIONAL TEACHER EVALUATION

The evaluation process for provisional teachers starts at the beginning of the school year with a one-week workshop to explain the process to new teachers. Development and evaluation of the provisional teacher is directed throughout the year by an advisory/assistance team consisting of the principal, the assistant principal for instruction (API), and a mentor teacher chosen by the administration. At an initial meeting, a teacher is asked to submit an Action Growth Plan to serve as the basis for his or her evaluation. This professional improvement plan must include specific individual goals consistent with district goals and must indicate what kinds of evidence the teacher will produce to document achievement. The advisory/assistance team assists, supports, and encourages the teacher in the development of and success in achieving the goals of the Action Growth Plan. It meets at least twice a semester for formative evaluation conferences on the teacher's total achievement.

The following guidelines are instrumental in assessing a teacher's progress toward stated system-wide and personal goals:

- Every provisional teacher must maintain a portfolio of evidence documenting successful performance as designated in the Action Growth Plan;
- Members of the advisory/assistance team conduct formal and informal observations using the CTPAS during the year;
- Mentors receive a one-half day of release time each month to observe and to confer with the teacher;
- Assistant principals for instruction observe and consult with each provisional teacher at least twice each month with regard to his or her progress;
- The principal is expected to spend at least half a day each semester with every provisional teacher in his or her school.

These expectations represent the district's designated minimums. More time may be allocated depending on the needs of the individual teacher. All observations are written and included in the teacher's portfolio. The activities of the advisory/assistance team remain constant throughout the school year.

The district has released twelve former classroom or coordinating teachers full time to conduct detailed assessments of teaching performance. They have received one month of intensive training on conducting classroom observations and preparing objective, accurate portrayals of classroom activities and teaching performance. During the second semester, three of these system-wide observer/evaluators conduct observations of each provisional teacher, the first one announced and the next two unannounced. Written reports of each observation are placed in the teacher's portfolio. Announced observations are routinely discussed with the teacher, but the teacher can also request a conference after an unannounced observation.

Observer/evaluators use CTPAS criteria to structure their observation comments. A script-tape of the lesson will serve as the data upon which summative judgments are based. The teacher receives a rating of 1 (bottom 10%) to 5 (top 10%) in each of the five CTPAS skill areas. Narrative statements justify the summative ratings given by the observer. Ratings of 3 or below represent a less-than-satisfactory performance.

For provisional teachers, training is part and parcel with the evaluation process. A variety of resources are at their disposal to aid them in their development during the year. All provisional teachers must attend classes on effective teaching after school or on Saturdays during the spring semester. Workshops on topics from assertive discipline to teaching reading in the content area are also available. APIs refer the teacher to materials in the system's Curriculum Resource Center and arrange for visitations to other classrooms to observe exemplary teaching techniques. Mentors serve as friendly critics, advisors, and role models throughout the year.

At the close of each semester, the advisory/assistance team must make a summative judgment on the provisional teacher's progress toward successful goal achievement and must extensively document the rating they give the teacher. Special attention must be given to those cases in which there are disagreements between the reports of observer/evaluators and the advisory/assistance team. In many cases the team will be more fully aware of contextual factors that may have influenced a given observation.

The team's recommendations facilitate contract renewal or termination at the end of the year. If the contract is renewed, the teacher retains provisional status for an additional year. In future years, the committee will have the option to terminate teachers, retain them under provisional status, or advance them to career nominee status. In the first year of the Career Development Program, options available to provisional teachers have enabled all experienced district teachers to receive the opportunity to achieve Career Level I status before any new teacher.

Any member of the advisory/assistance team may file a minority report. Though the responsibility and authority for all summative judgments rests with the advisory/assistance team, additional checks and balances insure the quality of the evaluations. Both an area-wide and a district-wide committee, served by teachers and administrators, review the recommendations of every team. In this fashion, the integrity of the system is insured.

CAREER CANDIDATE EVALUATION

While the basic structure of the evaluation process for career candidates is similar to that for provisional teachers, the requirements are more rigorous. Achieving the status of a Career Level I teacher certifies an individual's professional excellence and is accompanied by a $2,000 salary increase. Under North Carolina law, in future years the attainment of Career Level I status will also involve the awarding of tenure.

As with provisional teachers, each career candidate has an advisory/assistance team to assist and support him or her throughout the evaluation cycle. This team is composed of the principal, an API, and a colleague chosen by the teacher. Each candidate writes an Action Growth Plan similar to that asked of provisional teachers, but career candidates must focus on the demonstration of fourteen competencies. Rigorous measurement and documentation requirements are enforced. An area committee composed of the director of staff development and the five area program specialists, as well as the advisory/assistance team, are involved in reviewing and approving each improvement plan.

Members of the advisory/assistance team observe a teacher only at the teacher's request: It is assumed that as an experienced teacher, the candidate already possesses the instructional skills that form the basis of effective teaching. To verify the presence of these skills, three observer/evaluators conduct a total of nine formal observations of the teacher, six in the first semester and three in the second. Three observations are announced and six are unannounced. Conferences are scheduled only after announced observations, though, as with provisional teachers, conferences may be requested at any time. Written reports become part of the teacher's portfolio.

The teacher may meet with the advisory/assistance team at any time as he or she desires. Required meetings occur at the beginning of the year and the close of each semester. At this time, the team must make a summative judgment regarding the teacher's status for the following year. Based on the observation reports of the observer/evaluators and the documentation provided by the candidates in fulfilling the requirements of their action growth plans, the advisory/assistance teams may recommend either advancement to Career Level I status or continuation as career candidates. Teachers may voluntarily withdraw from the program if they wish.

Advancement to Career Level I status requires rigorous documentation. Advisory/assistance teams, for example, must specifically explain any rating below a 4 on any portion of their observation reports. The decisions of all advisory/assistance teams are reviewed both at the area and district level. The superintendent extends final approval.

Training resources available to career candidates are similar to those for provisional teachers. The advisory/assistance team attempts to provide whatever assistance they can. Both the API at the building level and the area program specialists at the district level work closely with career candidates to link them with the resources necessary for them to fulfill the requirements of their action growth plans.

Evaluation Outcomes

The first year (1984–1985) of implementation of the Career Development Program in Charlotte was a learning experience for teachers, building administrators, and central-office personnel. In some schools, the staff has developed a clear understanding of the goals and procedures of the evaluation program; in others there has been some confusion.

The majority of the district's professional staff believes that the program represents a positive means for accountability and improvement. Visitors are impressed with the enthusiasm of most participating teachers and administrators. There are some vocal critics of the Career Development Program, but this criticism seems based upon specific circumstances in particular schools.

As a result of the extensive feedback generated by the evaluation system, eighty-six of the district's 350 provisional teachers have voluntarily resigned. Some came to realize that they no longer wished to pursue a teaching career. Charlotte's director of career development estimates that 6% of the provisional teachers were induced to resign as a direct result of negative evaluative feedback. For example, in one school a teacher resigned the day before his mid-year summative evaluation conference, which he knew would be less than satisfactory. His major interest in teaching had been the opportunity to coach athletics; the focus of the evaluation process demonstrated his deficiencies in classroom instruction, and the efforts of his advisory/assistance team to provide help were unable to bring about appreciable improvement.

Of the 150 career candidates participating in the program, 137 reached Career Level I status. Five teachers voluntarily dropped out of the program during the school year, and six voluntarily agreed to extend their status as career candidates for a second year before going through the formal review process. Two individuals were denied Career Level I status at the end of the formal review process. That almost 10% did not achieve Career Level I status attests to the high standards and rigor with which the evaluation system has been applied.

Respondents at every level of the school system feel that the new evaluation process has focused their attention on instructional excellence in a meaningful way. According to one central-office administrator:

> I believe we've opened up the classroom door. Teachers are now excited about their professional growth. Those who have really tried to use this program as designed are getting excited and it's reducing the possibility of burnout.

At the individual school level, assistant principals for instruction agree that the new evaluation process has enabled them to perform their duties as coordinators of staff development and curricular resources much more than before:

> For the first time in twenty-nine years, we are saying things that should have been said all along, and we are making classroom expectations clear. I have never seen new teachers get as much support and help as has happened this year.

A principal at another school feels that the involvement of his staff in the Career Development Program as career candidates, provisional teachers, and members of advisory/assistance teams had a positive impact on collegial relations:

> I think we see better communication between teachers in the school [as a result of career development]. They talk to each other more . . . and professional topics characterize their discussion more often. It has been really exciting for me to see people that treat each other as colleagues.

Representatives of the local teachers' organizations also agree that the new evaluation process is a positive force in the district. A representative commented, "The main focus of the evaluation system is to help teachers improve . . . [but] if they do not improve, they are forced out of the system."

Teachers are somewhat divided in their assessment of the impact of the program on their instructional performance. Most complain about the stress of undergoing so many formal observations. For a few, the benefits of the evaluation process are not worth the cost. One provisional teacher, who received excellent ratings from an observer/evaluator, expects to leave this district and teach in another as a result of her stressful experience in the Career Development Program and the failure of her principal and API to support her.

Some teachers felt that evaluation provided an important "nudge" to their performance. One provisional teacher states:

> I believe I've really changed the way I teach as a result of the feedback I've gotten. . . . [The evaluation process] is motivating. It keeps me on my toes. You aren't allowed to be sloppy. . . . I think evaluation is an incentive that pushes you to improve.

While some teachers mention that evaluation is beneficial and "keeps them on their toes," for others, the evaluation process provides important feedback which validates the effectiveness of their classroom practice. In this respect, evaluation extends the notion of accountability not only to minimally competent teachers but to excellent teachers as well. To this point, a career candidate who had received excellent ratings from observer/evaluators states:

> I need the reassurance of people looking at what I am doing. If we are not looked at, we get the attitude that nobody cares. I think it can bring about a lack of motivation and I think this has happened to many teachers.

But beyond accountability, evaluation in Charlotte has stimulated teachers to examine carefully and to reflect on their actions in the classroom, making adjustments and improvements when areas of need become visible. Like holding up a mirror in the morning, evaluative feedback provides teachers glimpses of their performance which can serve as the basis for future improvement. A provisional teacher tells us:

Evaluation makes you think long and hard as you prepare for each lesson and makes you analyze what you are doing carefully. And I guess this wouldn't always be the case if you weren't participating in this program.

Another teacher, a career candidate who received excellent ratings from the observer/evaluators states:

I think [evaluation] made me more conscious about how I did things in my classroom. . . . I was much more conscious overall about my practice and I thought about my lessons more systematically. It helped me to avoid getting lazy.

These comments suggest that the evaluation component of the Career Development Program in Charlotte contributes to the achievement of both accountability and improvement goals for teachers of all effectiveness and experience levels.

PEER INVOLVEMENT

Peer involvement serves as the base of the formative component of the evaluation system. The assistant principal for instruction, along with the principal, the observer/evaluators, and the area and district review committees, provides a summative evaluation emphasis. The collegial support provided by mentor teachers insures that evaluations remain consistent with the norms and values of the classroom teachers themselves. Not surprisingly, AA team members often build a deep emotional attachment with the teachers with whom they work. Advisory/assistance team members believe that the performance of a teacher during an observer/ evaluator observation reflects their own professional competence. Peer involvement on advisory/assistance teams as well as district-wide review committees helps to insure that professional standards, not bureaucratic convenience, are a major aspect of the evaluation system.

One principal likens the role of the advisory/assistance team to that of a doctor who helps a woman through labor or to that of the unheralded offensive line of a football team:

The career candidates go through high and low periods during the year. But now the baby has finally arrived because we have completed the evaluation process, and as you would expect, we are all excited about that. It's been a long hard labor. The process here at this school has really been a team approach and the quarterback is the teacher. She calls the shots and we are the blockers that make it possible for her to be a winner.

Progress to Date

Implementing the new evaluation procedures in Charlotte-Mecklenburg for over 450 teachers has required special training for a large number of individuals—the participating teachers, principals, APIs, observer/evaluators, and advisory/assistance team members. This represented a tremendous financial burden to the district, and not all the significant actors in the evaluation process received adequate training. Mentors, for example, received no other training than a one-day workshop after the school year began and have consistently stated that they could benefit from more training. One mentor teacher in a high school comments:

> One wish that I have is that we had better instructions on how to rate the teacher when we observe them. I don't know what we're supposed to be doing. . . . Literally I was handed a form and told "Go observe and rate the teacher," and they handed me some sort of manual. I've had no training.

Several teachers have felt that advisory/assistance teams also could benefit from more training to clarify their role in the evaluation process. In several schools, both teachers and APIs are unclear about who has the ultimate responsibility for making a summative judgment on a teacher's performance.

But the remaining training need in the district represents a short-run problem. The Career Development Program has been designed so that career-level teachers will eventually occupy the roles of mentor and AA team members. As more teachers go through the evaluation process and attain Career Level I status, they will be able to fulfill these roles.

Though Charlotte-Mecklenburg's flexibility in implementing the Career Development Program represents a strength of the system, it has not been without its problems. Every career candidate has expressed frustration with the way the action growth plans have been handled: early in the year, area program specialists realized that the specificity and the length of action growth plans varied tremendously from building to building. In an effort to bring about some standardization, reduce paperwork, and clarify procedures, the district formed a committee to review and approve all action growth plans. Some career candidates have had to go through three iterations before their plans were finally approved.

New teachers, especially in secondary schools, have traditionally been expected to fulfill a variety of roles necessary to the school's total program. Coaching and club sponsorship, in particular, require large amounts of time in addition to that necessary for instructional planning. The additional demands of time and energy required by the evaluation process for provisional teachers creates a situation that many provisional teachers find difficult to cope with. APIs and provisional teachers have both commented that the district's demands on them were unreasonable. After-school commitments have often made it difficult for teachers to find time to meet with APIs or mentors to discuss instructional matters. States one provisional teacher who sponsored the cheerleaders and the junior class:

> I do need more time. After all, my primary goal and duty here at school is to teach. . . . But every time we have a work day they have some workshop we have to attend, but what I need is time to implement what I've learned already. I need time to think and work on these things.

The district's focus on instruction has thus created a dilemma for teachers and administrators alike. Provisional teachers must prioritize their responsibilities but are still expected to perform duties outside their normal classroom assignments. The district has not addressed this problem in any substantive manner to date.

Although Charlotte-Mecklenburg has relieved principals of a great deal of responsibility for teacher evaluation, they still remain key figures in implementing the evaluation process according to district plans. Not surprisingly, teachers' attitudes regarding the evaluation process vary depending on the school in which they teach and the commitment of their principal in insuring that the process is operating smoothly. The presence of observer/evaluators and area review committees establishes a certain amount of accountability, but principals' involvement in the career development process still varies appreciably. At some schools, principals spend as much as 30% of their time on teacher evaluation, while in others teachers have not talked with their principal at all regarding their progress through the evaluation process. While the responsibility for evaluation is dispersed among many individuals, a principal's lack of attention to evaluation sends a powerful message to teachers regarding the low priority he or she places on instruction. For example, one career candidate states:

If the principal is not involved in the evaluation process, teachers in the school probably won't see evaluation as being important. How the principal spends his time sends a powerful message to teachers about the priority that something has in the school. The principal serves as a symbol. If he arranges his schedule to spend time on [evaluation], then teachers get the message.

While the district steering committee chose to implement the career development plan for teachers first because they were most in need of the additional rewards attached to the process, plans exist to institute a Career Development Program for all professional staff in the district below the level of assistant superintendent. The additional accountability for principals that their participation in a career development evaluation process would introduce could have a significant impact on the manner in which teacher evaluation is implemented across the district.

Any innovation of the scale of the Career Development Program requires time before its ultimate impact can be assessed. Six years must pass before Charlotte's staged implementation plan installs the entire program. Some aspects of the program have yet to be specified—for example, descriptions of duties, selection, and evaluation procedure for Career Level II and III teachers have not yet been developed.

Effects of the process on student achievement, teacher turnover, and community support for education are yet to be determined. Yet positive comments by teachers and administrators regarding the first year of the new evaluation process outnumber the negative ones by a three-to-one margin. In every instance, negative comments result when the program is not being implemented as planned. Leadership by a principal committed to the Career Development Program seems to be a key to success.

References

Argyris, C. *Reasoning, Learning, and Action.* San Francisco: Jossey Bass, 1982.

Armor, D., P. Conry-Osequera, M. Cox, N. King, L. McDonnell, A. Pascal, E. Pauly, and G. Zellman. *Analysis of the School Preferred Reading Program.* Santa Monica: Rand Corporation, 1977.

Berman, P., and M. W. McLaughlin. *Federal Programs Supporting Educational Change.* R–1589–HEW. Santa Monica: Rand Corporation, 1978.

Bridges, E. *The Incompetent Teacher: The Challenge and the Response.* San Francisco: Falmer Press, 1986.

Educational Research Service. *Evaluating Teacher Performance.* Arlington, Va.: Educational Research Service, 1978.

Etzioni, A. *A Comparative Analysis of Complex Organizations.* New York: Free Press, 1975.

Fullan, M. "Performance Appraisal and Curriculum Implementation Research." Paper presented at Conference on Performance Appraisal for Effective Schooling, Ontario Institute for the Study of Education, Toronto, Ontario, Canada, February 27–28, 1986.

Glidewell, J. C., and T. McLean. "Professional Support Systems: The Teaching Profession." In *Applied Research in Help-Seeking and Reactions to Aid,* edited by A. Madler, J. D. Fisher, and B. M. Paulo, New York: Academic Press, 1983.

Good, T. "Research on Classroom Teaching." In *Handbook on Teaching and Policy,* edited by L. Shulman and G. Sykes, 42–80. New York: Longman, 1983.

Herndon, J. *Notes From a Schoolteacher.* New York: Simon & Schuster, 1985.

Hyde, A. A., and D. R. Moore. *Making Sense of Staff Development: An Analysis of Staff Development Programs and Their Costs in Three Urban School Districts.* Washington, D.C.: U.S. Government Printing Office, 1982.

Kanter, R. M. *Changemaster.* New York: Simon & Schuster, 1984.

Kerr, S. and J. W. Slocum, Jr. "Controlling the Performances of People in Organizations." In *Handbook of Organizational Design,* edited by W. H. Starbuck. Oxford: Oxford University Press, 1981.

Lacey, C. *The Socialization of Teachers.* London: Methuen, 1977.

Lawton, S. B., E. S. Hickox, K. A. Leithwood, and D. F. Musella. *Performance Appraisal of Certificated Education Staff in Ontario School Boards.* Toronto, Canada: Non-Technical Report, Ontario Ministry of Education, 1985.

Levinthal, B., and J. G. March. "A Model of Adaptive Organizational Search." *Journal of Economic Behavior and Organization* 2 (1982): 307–333.

Lewin, K. *The Conceptual Representation and the Measurement of Psychological Forces.* Durham, N.C.: Duke University Press, 1938.

Little, J. *School Success and Staff Development: The Role of Staff Development in Urban Desegregated Schools.* Boulder, Colo.: Center for Action Research, 1981.

Lortie, D. C. "The Balance of Control and Autonomy in Elementary School Teaching." In *The Semi-Professions and Their Organization.* Edited by A. Etzioni. New York: Free Press, 1969.

Lortie, D. C. *Schoolteacher.* Chicago: University of Chicago Press, 1975.

Lundberg, C. C. "On the Feasibility of Cultural Intervention in Organizations." In *Organizational Culture,* edited by P. J. Frost, L. F. Moore, M. R. Louis, C. C. Lundberg, and J. Martin, 169–185. Beverly Hills, Calif.: Sage Publications, 1985.

McGreal, T. L. *Successful Teacher Evaluation.* Alexandria, Va.: Association for Supervision and Curriculum Development, 1983.

McLaughlin, M. W., R. S. Pfeifer, D. Swanson-Owens, and S. Yee. "Why Teachers Won't Teach." *Phi Delta Kappan,* 67, February 1986, pp. 420–426.

McLaughlin, M., and P. Shields. "Involving Parents in the Schools: Lessons for Policy." Paper presented at the Conference on Effects of Alternative Designs in Compensatory Education, Washington, D.C., June 1986.

Meyer, J. W., and B. Rowan. "Institutionalized Organizations: Formal Structure as Myth and Ceremony." *American Journal of Sociology* 83 (1977): 340–363.

Peterson, C. H. *A Century's Growth in Teacher Evaluation in the United States.* New York: Vantage Press, 1982.

Sabatier, P., and D. Mazmanian. "The Implementation of Public Policy: A Framework for Analysis." *Policy Studies Journal* 8 (4) (1980).

Schlechty, P. C., and D. Crowell. *Understanding and Managing Staff Development in an Urban School System.* Final Report, Contract 400–79–0056. Washington, D.C.: National Institute of Education, 1982.

Schon, D. A. *Beyond the Stable State.* New York: Random House, 1971.

Schon, D. A. *The Reflective Practitioner: How Professionals Think in Action.* New York: Basic Books, 1983.

Southern Regional Education Board. *Career Ladder Clearinghouse.* Atlanta, Ga.: Southern Regional Education Board, December 1986.

Stiggins, R. J., and N. Bridgeford. "Performance Assessment for Teacher Development." *Educational Evaluation and Policy Analysis* 7, (1) (1985).

Travers, R.M. W. "Criteria of Good Teaching." In *Handbook of Teacher Evaluation,* edited by J. Millman. Beverly Hills: Sage, 1981.

Wildavsky, A. *Speaking Truth to Power,* (Chap. 9, "The Self-Evaluating Organization"). Boston: Little Brown, 1979.

Wise, A. E., L. Darling-Hammond, M. W. McLaughlin, and H. T. Bernstein. *Teacher Evaluation: A Study of Effective Practices.* Santa Monica, Calif.: Rand Corporation: June 1984.

Index

About the Authors

Milbrey Wallin McLaughlin is an associate professor of education at Stanford University. Her research interests focus on planned change in education, intergovernmental relations, the organizational context of teaching, and evaluation. Prior to joining the Stanford faculty, she was a policy analyst with the Rand Corporation, where her research centered on federal and state efforts to promote educational change and improvement.

Richard Scott Pfeifer is a high school administrator for the Howard County Public School System in Columbia, Maryland. He is completing his doctoral studies in Administration and Policy Analysis at the School of Education, Stanford University. His research interests focus on organizational theory, teacher evaluation, and leadership in education.